Men-at-Arms • 434

World War II German Police Units

Gordon Williamson · Illustrated by Gerry Embleton

Series editor Martin Windrow

First published in Great Britain in 2006 by Osprey Publishing
Midland House, West Way, Botley, Oxford OX2 0PH, UK
443 Park Avenue South, New York, NY 10016, USA
Email: info@ospreypublishing.com

ISBN-10: 1 84603 068 4
ISBN-13: 978 1 84603 068 0

Editor: Martin Windrow
Page layouts by Alan Hamp
Typeset in Helvetica Neue and ITC New Baskerville
Index by Glyn Sutcliffe
Originated by PPS Grasmere, Leeds, UK
Printed in China through World Print Ltd.

06 07 08 09 10   10 9 8 7 6 5 4 3 2 1

A CIP catalogue record for this book is available from the British Library

FOR A CATALOGUE OF ALL BOOKS PUBLISHED BY
OSPREY MILITARY AND AVIATION PLEASE CONTACT:
North America:
Osprey Direct c/o Random House Distribution Center, 400 Hahn Road, Westminster, MD 21157, USA
Email: info@ospreydirect.com

All other regions:
Osprey Direct UK PO Box 140, Wellingborough, Northants, NN8 2FA, UK
Email: info@ospreydirect.co.uk

Buy online at www.ospreypublishing.com

Photographic credit

Unless otherwise indicated, all images are from the author's collection.

Editor's Note

As always when describing World War II insignia, the terms 'silver' and 'gold' refer to cheap alloys having the appearance of those metals. In most German insignia, stamped aluminium and aluminium wire thread were used to simulate silver. The few examples of actual plated metal are referred to as e.g. 'silvered'. For simplicity, some German compound terms which normally take a hyphen have been separated to e.g. Hochgebirgs Gendarmerie, etc.

Artist's Note

Readers may care to note that the original paintings from which the colour plates in this book were prepared are available for private sale. All reproduction copyright whatsoever is retained by the Publishers. All enquiries should be addressed to:

Time Machine SA, La Chaine 15, Prêles, CH-2515 Switzerland

The Publishers regret that they can enter into no correspondence upon this matter.

WORLD WAR II GERMAN POLICE UNITS

INTRODUCTION

THE POLICE HAD ALWAYS HAD a respected status in German society. This may in part have been due to the fact that German policemen had traditionally been recruited fairly heavily from among former soldiers, and even before the advent of the Nazis were a paramilitary rather than a purely civilian force.

After World War I, the Treaty of Versailles had limited Germany to an army of 100,000 men, which resulted in huge numbers of wartime soldiers being thrown into unemployment. There were no such restrictions on the size of the police forces, however, and considerable numbers of former soldiers simply moved from one uniformed service to another. Under the precarious conditions of the Weimar Republic, when the greatest threat to the authority and integrity of the state was perceived as coming from the Communist movement, the government was quite happy to see the police strengthened by an influx of such men, who tended to hold authoritarian views about society's overriding need for 'order'. The military also saw the benefit of keeping large numbers of trained and disciplined men within the control of an organ of the state, providing a cadre who might at some future date be transferred back to the authority of the armed forces.

Inevitably, when the Nazis came to power at the end of January 1933, they were happy to continue with this expansion and militarization of the police. For years they had been quietly infiltrating the police forces of the various German states or Länder, and many Nazi Party members were already in senior positions. Now these officers were empowered to begin combing out policemen whom they felt to be politically unreliable, and any with known democratic sympathies were ousted. Almost immediately after the Nazis came to power, members of the police were seen wearing the Party's swastika armband on their uniforms.

The police structure at this point was still organized on a state-by-state basis. In Hitler's first cabinet, Hermann Göring was appointed as chief ('President') of the Prussian Police, thus gaining control of the largest and most influential of such forces. Within weeks, Department IA of the Prussian Landespolizei had been completely

Heinrich Himmler, the Reichsführer-SS, held the newly created post of Chef der Deutschen Polizei from April 1934. He spared no effort to ensure that the SS controlled – directly or indirectly – every important policing function in the Third Reich, to the extent that eventually even the most humble Police functionary carried an SS paybook.

purged of any suspect elements, and its Amt III was retitled as the Geheime Staats Polizei – the Secret State Police or Gestapo.

The numbers of police available to the government in Berlin were quickly doubled by Göring's creation of the Prussian Hilfspolizei or police auxiliaries to assist the force in maintaining order. These were generally members of the Sturmabteilung (SA) with a smaller number of members of the Allgemeine–SS, and others recruited from war veterans' associations, who could be trusted to support the new and still not fully established regime.[1] Similar Hilfspolizei units were created throughout the other German Länder within a matter of days; they wore the uniforms of their parent organizations, if any, with a white 'Hilfspolizei' armband. These auxiliaries were disbanded in August 1933 – partly due to foreign protests that they contravened the terms of the Versailles Treaty, but also because Hitler was already becoming uneasy over his ability to control the SA, which provided the greater part of the Hilfspolizei.

Although short-lived, the Hilfspolizei had served their purpose in helping to ensure the survival of the Nazi government in the first shaky days of its existence, when it was still battling things out in the streets against strong Communist and socialist movements.

In January 1934, by now more confident, the regime began to unify the Landespolizei forces by transferring police powers to the national – Reichs – level; and from this point on in this text it is logical to capitalize the name of the service as 'Police'. The post of Chief of the German Police in the Ministry of the Interior was created, and with Heinrich Himmler's appointment to this post in April 1934 the blurring of lines between the Police and the SS began. Himmler would ensure that the majority of senior and middle-level Police posts were filled by men who were also members of the SS and thus owed obedience to him. The new national Police apparatus that he controlled was divided into two major elements: the Ordnungspolizei (Order Police, Orpo) and the Sicherheitspolizei (Security Police, Sipo – into which the Gestapo was absorbed).

When Germany's rearmament and the formation of the new Wehrmacht (armed forces) were openly declared in March 1935, many thousands of policemen were transferred to the Army, including those still serving who were perceived as lacking in enthusiasm for the Nazi regime. Senior ranks who remained in the Police and who were not already members of the SS were pressured into joining; membership became a prerequisite for a successful Police career. (It is interesting to note, however, that at the outbreak of war in September 1939 only some 15 per cent of the membership of the Gestapo were actually members of the SS.)

On the outbreak of war the manpower needs of the armed forces led to the conscription of many younger, fitter policemen; consequently, numbers of older men not considered fit for military service were taken into the Police as reservists 'for the duration' – and some of these were the very men who had been purged for perceived political unreliability between 1933 and 1935. Although the 'Nazification' of the Police may have thus been somewhat diluted, it is unlikely that these men had much influence; their reputation for limited political loyalty would certainly

A member of a Landespolizei force, wearing an M1916 steel helmet and a uniform dating from before the unification of the police forces; note the star badge on his belt buckle, and the absence of a Police national emblem on the left sleeve. Many of the German states had their own unique police uniforms and insignia, which would be swept away when the new grey-green national uniform was introduced in the mid-1930s.
(Josef Charita)

1 See MAA 213, *The SA 1921–45: Hitler's Stormtroopers*, and MAA 266, *The Allgemeine-SS*

have remained on their records, and they would continue to be regarded as suspect.

From 1942, dual Police and SS ranks were adopted by Police generals, who from then on would wear SS-pattern rank insignia, albeit in Police colours. Police personnel were also issued with pay books (Soldbücher) bearing the SS runes rather than the Police eagle on the cover.

As time passed, the Police, rather than providing the Army with manpower as originally envisaged, began to field its own rifle regiments and even light armoured units, to serve behind the military front lines in the occupied territories. Although many of these units were engaged in actions against heavily armed partisans, others were attached to SD Einsatzgruppen and used in sweeps through the civilian populations, rounding up Jews and other 'undesirables'. It has now been well documented that the German Police – although still maintaining tens of thousands of personnel on regular, traditional duties in Germany – became deeply involved in some of the worse excesses of the Nazi regime.

At the end of the war, the need for the overstretched Allied armies to maintain law and order in the chaotic situation which prevailed in Germany meant that in most cases only a cursory review of the conduct of individual Police personnel during the Third Reich was made, in order to weed out the worst offenders. Many Police officers were simply allowed to go back on duty without any meaningful scrutiny of their wartime records.

* * *

Few organizations during the period of the Third Reich came close to the levels of complexity of the German Police, and that complexity has resulted in a dearth of available reference material in any manageable form.

A full list of the different functions in the various German Länder totals 34, including everything from Forestry and Foodstuffs Police to Lodging and Pathways Police. While this may seem wildly excessive, it should be recalled that many of these functions also existed in most other countries. The principal difference was that whereas in Germany they were performed by the Police, elsewhere they tended to be carried out by regulatory officials of various municipal authorities, since many related simply to administrative and licensing functions. Nevertheless, it is unsurprising that when the Nazis came to power they wished to rationalize and unify the numerous policing functions throughout the various Länder. Despite Germany possessing such a huge range of police functions, it is worth pointing out that the total number of policemen in the country at that time was under 150,000 – significantly less than in Great Britain or France.

To cover the entire German Police apparatus would require a significant multi-volume work – indeed, at the time of writing such an

Members of the Berlin Schutzpolizei parade under the Brandenburg Gate led by a mounted officer. He wears a shako plume, silver cord aiguilettes, and brocade waist and pouch belts; the enlisted men have plumes and wear white belts. In parade order the enlisted ranks wore grey gloves, the warrant officers (the most senior NCO grades) and officers white. Note that the policemen march with slung rifles, the officers with drawn swords. (Josef Charita)

Kurt Daluege (1897–1946), in the rank of SS-Oberstgruppenführer und Generaloberst der Polizei – see Plate G3. In 1934 this former chief of the Berlin SS and Police became the national Chef der Ordnungspolizei, answering directly to Himmler, which he remained in name even after his executive duties were taken over by SS-Obgruf u. Genobst der Polizei Alfred Wunnenberg in June 1942. Daluege owed his position to his absolute loyalty rather than to any great ability; a heavy drinker, he was considered slow-witted, and behind his back his colleagues called him 'Dummi-dummi'. In June 1942 he replaced the assassinated Reinhard Heydrich as 'Protector of Bohemia-Moravia' – the Nazi proconsul in occupied Czechoslovakia, where he presided over the atrocious reprisals for his predecessor's assassination. He was hanged in Prague in 1946.

in-depth study is being prepared in the USA. Meanwhile it is hoped that this small introductory work will give some insight into the structure, responsibilities and uniform distinctions of the German Order Police.[2]

STRUCTURE

Ordnungspolizei (Orpo)
Schutzpolizei des Reiches (National Protection Police)
Schutzpolizei der Gemeinden (Municipal Protection Police)
Gendarmerie (Rural Police)
Verwaltungspolizei (Administrative Police)
Kolonialpolizei (Colonial Police)
Wasserschutzpolizei (Water Protection Police)
Feuerschutzpolizei (Fire Protection Police)
Feuerwehren (fire brigades, auxiliary Fire Protection Police)
Luftschutzpolizei (Air Protection Police)
Technische Nothilfe (Technical Emergency Service)
Polizei Fliegerstaffeln (Police Flying Units – liaison and transport)
Sonderpolizei (Special Police units not directly under control of Hauptamt Orpo, including:)
Bahnschutzpolizei (Railway Protection Police)
Reichsbahnfahndungsdienst (Railway Criminal Investigation Dept)
Postschutz (Postal Protection)
Funkschutz (Broadcast Protection)
Bergpolizei (Mines Police)
Deichpolizei (Dyke & Dams Police)
Hilfspolizei (Auxiliary Police)

Command structure: Hauptamt Orpo

The national command office for the Ordnungspolizei was in Berlin. The position of Chef der Ordnungspolizei was originally held by SS-Oberstgruppenführer und Generaloberst der Polizei Kurt Daluege, replaced in 1943 by SS-Obergruppenführer und General der Polizei Alfred Wunnenberg. Although Daluege remained the senior officer, to all intents and purposes operational control of the Orpo after this date passed to Wünnenberg. The Order Police Main Office was divided into numerous senior and subordinate departments or Ämter:

Amt I – Kommandoamt. Headed by SS-Brigadeführer und Generalmajor der Polizei Anton Diermann until late 1944, when Diermann was replaced by SS-Brigaf u. Genmaj der Polizei Hans Flade. This Command department was further subdivided into three subordinate Amtsgruppen:

2 For the military and security police organs not covered in this title, see MAA 213, *German Military Police Units 1939–45*, and Warrior 61, *German Security & Police Soldier 1939–45*

Amtsgruppe I comprised sub-offices covering aspects such as finance, clothing, training, ordnance, equipment, etc.

Amtsgruppe II was responsible for personnel matters as well as ideological training.

Amtsgruppe III was the Police medical department.

Amt II – *Verwaltung und Recht.* Headed by SS-Gruppenführer und General der Polizei Ministerialdirektor Dr Werner Bracht, this Administrative & Rights department was also divided into three Amtsgruppen:

Amtsgruppe I was responsible for pay and allowances, pensions, budgeting, the Police legal code, and other administrative matters.

Amtsgruppe II covered registration and control of the population, theatres, cinemas and places of entertainment, trades and handicrafts, and traffic control.

Amtsgruppe III dealt with Police billeting and accommodation.

Amt III – *Wirtschaftsverwaltungsamt.* Headed by SS-Obergruppenführer und Generalleutnant der Waffen-SS und Polizei August Frank, this Economic department was subdivided into four Amtsgruppen dealing with clothing and rations, finance and pay, quartering and billeting, and pensions and allowances. A fifth subsection also dealt with personnel matters.

Amt IV – *Technische Nothilfe* Headed by SS-Gruf u. Genlt der Polizei Willy Schmelcher, this branch was the technical emergency service of the SS and Police – effectively, its Engineering branch.

Amt V – *Feuerwehren* This was the fire brigades bureau, headed by Genmaj der Polizei Schnell.

Amt VI – *Kolonialpolizei* The colonial police, headed by SS-Ogruf u. Gen der Waffen-SS u. Polizei Karl von Pfeffer-Wildenbruch.

Amt VII – *Technisches SS und Polizeiakademie* The SS and Police technical training academy, headed by SS-Brigaf u. Genmaj der Polizei Prof Dr Hellmuth Gerloff.

As well as these main administrative offices, Hauptamt Orpo also included various inspectorates, and supervised many training schools.

Territorial organization

Since 1919 Germany's national territory had been divided into 'military districts' or Wehrkreise, numbered in Roman numerals – e.g. Wehrkreis III, with headquarters in Berlin, covered the Altmark, Neumark and Brandenburg. Their primary purpose had been as Army divisional recruitment and training commands, but with the creation of a unified state Police service its territorial structure was grafted on to this existing organization. In each Wehrkreis a Befehlshaber der Ordnungspolizei (BdO – Senior Order Police Commander) was appointed as the representative of the Hauptamt Orpo and of the regional Höhere SS und

In conversation with an Allgemeine-SS officer, a scarred Police colonel, Oberst Dr Nozieff (right), wears walking-out uniform with straight trousers and shoes. The sabre is of an earlier style used before the introduction of the *Polizei Degen*, but the photo shows the suspension strap emerging from under the pocket flap. The fine quality of the officer's collar patches, and the hand-embroidered aluminium wire Police national emblem worn on the left sleeve, is evident. The peaked service cap has officer's silver chin cords. (Josef Charita)

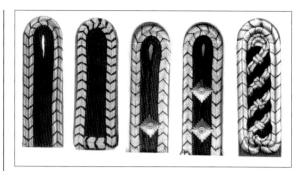

Polizei Führer (Higher SS & Police Leader). Amongst the staff allocated to the BdO was the Polizei Schulungsleiter; this individual equated roughly to the Soviet political commissar, with the task of ensuring that Police personnel were fully indoctrinated in the tenets of Nazism. Below the BdO in the organizational structure were a number of Kommandeure der Orpo, who answered to the BdO for the control of various sub-units of the Ordnungspolizei within a district or region.

Police enlisted ranks' shoulder straps: (left to right) Wachtmeister (1936–41), Oberwachtmeister (1941–45), Revieroberwachtmeister (1936–41), Hauptwachtmeister (1936–41), and Meister (1936–45). The cord across the base of NCOs' straps – see second left – was only added in 1941. The outer cords were analogous to the *Tresse* on Wehrmacht shoulder straps. Although some minor branches had their own designs, the great majority of Police organizations used these patterns, with variations of colour. The inner cords are of wool in the uniform facing colour – here, as most often, brown; the outer cords are of silver (aluminium, either bright or matt) flecked with chevrons of brown; the rank 'pips' are aluminium; and all are worked on underlays of *Truppenfarbe*. The Wasserschutzpolizei differed slightly in that the basic 'facing colour' inner cords and the *Truppenfarbe* underlay were both bright yellow.

Police ranks

Before looking individually at the multifarious branches of the German Police, we list here their rank sequence, which mostly followed the same basic system. Rank titles in each of the diverse branches normally consisted of the basic rank designation followed by a suffix indicating the exact branch, e.g. Meister der Schutzpolizei, Hauptmann der Gendarmerie, etc. Ranks are listed from junior to senior:

Police rank	Military equivalent where appropriate
Polizei Anwärter	(Private soldiers)
Unterwachtmeister	Unteroffizier
Wachtmeister	Unterfeldwebel
Oberwachtmeister	Feldwebel
Revierwachtmeister	–
Hauptwachtmeister	Oberfeldwebel
Meister	–
Obermeister	–

The officer rank titles, from Leutnant up to Generaloberst der Polizei, mirrored those of the Army and Air Force.

POLICE INSIGNIA:
Collar patches

For all enlisted ranks these were woven on a base of the colour identifying the wearer's branch, with silver-grey thread *Litzen* – the traditional German Army 'Guard lace' bars; the patches were edged with narrow silver-grey cord all round. For officer ranks, hand-embroidered silver wire *Litzen* were worked on a wool base in the branch colour, without cord edging. The base colours or *Truppenfarben* – equivalent to military *Waffenfarben* – were as follows:

Schutzpolizei – bright 'police-green'
Schutzpolizei der Gemeinden – wine-red
Gendarmerie – orange
Feuerschutzpolizei – carmine-red
Wasserschutzpolizei – bright yellow
Verwaltungspolizei – light grey

Medical and veterinary personnel wore cornflower-blue and black respectively.

General officers initially wore collar patches in the same style as those of the Army, but with the 'alt Larisch' embroidery worked in gold thread on a police-green rather than a red base. In early 1942 Police

generals were authorized new insignia based on the SS pattern, but executed in gold on police-green rather than silver on black, as follows:
SS-Brigadeführer und Generalmajor der Polizei – three oak leaves
SS-Gruppenführer u. Generalleutnant der Polizei – plus one 'pip'
SS-Obergruppenführer u. General – plus two pips
SS-Oberstgruppenführer u. Generaloberst – plus three pips.

Shoulder straps

For junior enlisted ranks and NCOs, shoulder straps of rank differed markedly from those of the Army, Air Force and Waffen-SS. They were made on a base underlay of the appropriate *Truppenfarbe* which showed around the edges, but were of a bewildering variety. The basic design showed an inner core of four straight cords or braids in an appropriate solid colour – usually the uniform facing colour, so dark brown for the bulk of the Orpo – around which were two outer lengths of cord flecked with a fine chevron design. For the most junior ranks these outer cords were in the same colour as the central cord, with silver chevrons; for the Wachtmeister grades they were in silver flecked with facing-coloured chevrons. Senior NCOs or warrant officers – the Meister grades – wore straps with interwoven facing-coloured and chevron-flecked silver cords in the centre, in a diagonal pattern, surrounded by the usual chevron-flecked silver outer cords.

Ranks were indicated as described below, from junior to senior. Police ranks, like those of many other organizations, were revised at various times during the war, and the ranks listed here represent the final system, from the mid-point of the war onwards:
Polizei Anwärter – plain strap as described above
Unterwachtmeister – plain strap as above
Rottwachtmeister – as above, with silver braid loop around base
Wachtmeister – silver/chevron-fleck outer cords
Oberwachtmeister – silver/chevron-fleck outer cords around sides and base
Revieroberwachtmeister – as above, plus single silver pip
Hauptwachtmeister – as above, with two silver pips
Meister – diagonal interwoven central cords, facing colour and silver/chevron fleck, outer cords silver/chevron fleck.
Officer ranks wore military-pattern shoulder straps, with silver cords on an underlay in *Truppenfarbe*, and gilt rank pips:
Leutnant – straight silver cords on coloured underlay
Oberleutnant – as above, with single gilt pip
Hauptmann – as above, with two pips
Major – interwoven silver cords on coloured underlay
Oberstleutnant – as above, with single pip
Oberst – as above, with two pips
Generalmajor – interwoven gold/silver cords

A Hauptwachtmeister of Schutzpolizei supervises the installation of a sign showing the direction of the nearest air raid shelter ('Zum öffentlichen/ Luftschutzraum', with a red arrow). Note the enlisted ranks' peaked service cap with a leather chin strap; the enlisted ranks' collar patches with cord edging; the Police national emblem on the left sleeve, with a location name embroidered above in an arc; the large, unpleated skirt pockets of the tunic; the fine quality of his boots, more like officers' riding boots than soldiers' marching boots; and the Police dress bayonet, with its aluminium brocade *Troddel* shot with lines of black and red. (Joseph Charita)

A Police junior NCO in the mid- or late war years, wearing the grey-green field cap, and the M1943 field blouse issued to replace the more elaborate Police tunic – the contrast in shades suggests that this tunic is in Army field-grey. The cap was of the shape used by the Wehrmacht services other than the Army. From 1942 the top edge of the flap was piped in *Truppenfarbe*, but this example shows the earlier Y-shape of the green piping which followed both crests of the top fold and passed vertically down the front of the crown. The Police national emblem is machine-woven in silver-grey on black. Note that the collar *Litzen* are applied directly to the collar, without coloured base patches or silver-grey edging. (Josef Charita)

Generalleutnant – as above, with single large silvered pip
General der Polizei – as above, with two pips
Generaloberst der Polizei – as above, with three smaller pips

Sleeve eagles

All enlisted ranks wore a machine-embroidered Police-style national emblem of a wreathed eagle-and-swastika on the left upper sleeve. This was in the *Truppenfarbe* for their branch, except for a black swastika, and worked on a backing of their uniform colour. For officer ranks the eagle was hand-embroidered in silver thread, and for general officers it was worked in gold-coloured thread.

Enlisted ranks' eagles would often have the district name embroidered in an arc above, though this was not universal, and was supposed to be removed in rural areas in late 1941.

Runes

Members of the Police who were also members of the SS were authorized to display a set of embroidered SS-runes low on the left breast, in silver-grey or silver on a uniform-coloured backing.

ORDNUNGSPOLIZEI EXECUTIVE BRANCHES

The Ordnungspolizei may be considered as sub-divided into two main branches: the executive branch – the regular uniformed Police – and the administrative branch. The organizations embraced by the executive branch were the following:

SCHUTZPOLIZEI DES REICHES

The Schutzpolizei (Schupo) were the regular uniformed Police stationed in the larger towns and cities. For smaller communities a specific number of men were allocated dependent on the population size, ranging from one policeman for a populace of 2,000, to six for a populace of 10,000. Thereafter, manpower allocation was on a 'per head of population' basis; for instance, in areas with a population of up to 20,000, one policeman was allocated for every 1,000 inhabitants.

The basic Schupo organization was at precinct level. Each precinct (Reviere) covered between 20,000 and 30,000 inhabitants, with a police station manned by 20 to 40 officers who would patrol their local 'beats'. A number of such precincts would be grouped together administratively to form a section or Abschnit. In very large cities a number of such Abschnitte could be administered as a Gruppe. The Schutzpolizei Abschnitte were under the control of a Kommandeur der Schutzpolizei for that city. This local commander would be under the direct control of the Polizeipräsident, who commanded not only the Schupo but all police organizations for his area.

In addition to the manpower allocated to precinct stations, the Schutzpolizei maintained 'Barracked Police' units or Kasernierte Polizeieinheiten. These were organized into companies of approximately 100 men (referred to as Hundertschaften, prior to the adoption of the military term Kompanie). When the situation required, these independent companies could be assembled into battalions on the authority of senior commanders such as the BdO. Their duties included providing guards (in conjunction with local SS units) for major party gatherings; dealing with 'internal unrest'; preventing looting, and maintaining order and traffic flow after air raids or any other major catastrophes. To give an idea of the scale of such units, it is estimated that during the Anschluss with Austria in 1938 around 150 such Barracked Police companies were mobilized, representing some 15,000 men.

Schupo combat units

With the outbreak of war, the Police formed a considerable number of rifle battalions (certainly in excess of 80), each consisting of more than 500 men. These were sent out of Germany to operate behind the front line combat units of the Wehrmacht, with the tasks of preventing partisan activity and sabotage, securing lines of communication, guarding installations, and generally maintaining law and order. Manpower was made available for such units by drafting in large numbers of Police reservists to form additional battalions. Unfortunately, as already noted, the activities of Schutzpolizei units in the occupied countries went far beyond what might be considered legitimate security operations.

On the Eastern Front other Police units became embroiled in front line combat against regular Red Army troops, and despite their small size and light armament they sometimes acquitted themselves well in battle – an obvious example being those which fought in the defence of the Kholm Pocket in 1942.

During 1941 so many Police units were already in the field in the East that they were assembled into regiments; 28 of these were formed, each of three battalions, giving a total of well over 46,000 men. As the war dragged on nine more such regiments were formed, now known as Polizei Schützen Regimenter – 'Police rifle regiments'. In 1943, all such regiments were renamed as SS-Polizei (Schützen) Regimenter.

These units consisted of Schupo personnel with relatively good levels of fitness and training. Those less able or more elderly reservists (often over 50 years of age) who were called up into the Barracked Police remained in Germany, where they were formed into Polizei Wachbataillone or 'guard battalions', to perform duties such as maintaining order in areas heavily affected by bombing. These Wachbataillone were of negligible value as combatants against advancing Allied units.

Subordinate support and service units

There were a number of smaller units which might be available to the local Kommandeur der Schutzpolizei for particular duties, including:

Schutzpolizei NCOs in parade dress. All three in the front rank are decorated former soldiers displaying the Iron Cross, and two of them wear the Wound Badge; equally, all three seem to wear the bronze *SA-Wehrabzeichen*. Many former Army men joined the Landespolizei after World War I. (Josef Charita)

Kraftfahbereitschaften Motor vehicle maintenance crews.

Motoriserte Verkehrsbereitschaften The great majority of Police activity was carried out on foot, but these motorized units provided fast response patrol cars and motorcycle/sidecar combinations.

Verkehrsunfallbereitschaften These were motorized fast response units, but for reacting to traffic accidents rather than crimes; they might be equipped with specialized vehicles such as tow trucks.

Verkehrskompanie (mot.) zbV These units, created late in 1941, were tasked with control of wartime traffic; they made spot checks to ensure that vehicles were roadworthy and were being lawfully used under the various wartime restrictions.

Polizei Nachrichtenstaffeln These maintained Police communications networks – radio and telephone systems, fixed and mobile transmitters, etc.

Polizei Reiterstaffeln A small number of independent mounted units existed. In most areas, when required, the mounted Police worked in mixed patrols alongside regular Schupo foot policemen.

Motorisierte Überfallkommandos The Police riot squads, on hand to quell civil unrest or to carry out other emergency work. Given the nature of the regime, anti-government demonstrations inside Germany on such a scale as to require the use of such troops were, to say the least, unusual. They were equipped with light armoured cars armed with machine guns. Although not seeing much use within the Reich, they were deployed in occupied territories to assist in anti-partisan operations.

Sanitätsdienst Each area had its own Sanitätsstelle or first aid centre to provide treatment to injured policemen.

Veterinärdienst The Police maintained their own veterinary service to provide care and treatment to their horses and police dogs.

* * *

The regular uniformed Schupo received plain clothes assistance from within and outside their own ranks. Some would occasionally don civilian clothing for undercover patrols – these were distinct from the Kriminal Polizei (equivalent to the British CID), who operated in plain clothes all the time.

One of the major sources of assistance to the Police was the Nazi Party's own motorized branch, the NSKK (National Sozialistisches Kraftfahr Korps). The NSKK had its own Verkehrsdienst or traffic control service which was often employed as an auxiliary traffic police force – not only in Germany but also in the occupied territories, including what were effectively combat zones on the Eastern Front and in North Africa.

Other assistance came from the Hitler Jugend.[3] As early as 1934 the Hitler Youth formed its own patrol service (HJ-Streifendienst), initially to maintain order and discipline within the HJ, but also to prevent unruly behaviour by other

This Revieroberwachtmeister wears the M1943 field blouse and peaked field cap; the latter may show *Truppenfarbe* piping at the crown seam, and certainly has the white metal Police eagle pinned below the machine-woven national cockade. Note the contrasting black swastika on the bright green sleeve eagle; and the bar of chevron-flecked silver cord obviously added retrospectively across the base of his shoulder straps, which also bear a pin-on cipher above the rank pip. His status as an Eastern Front combat veteran is unmistakable: he displays the ribbons of the Iron Cross Second Class and the Eastern Winter Campaign 1941/42 medal, a General Assault Badge and a black Wound Badge.

3 See Warrior 102, *The Hitler Youth 1933–45*

youths (including drinking or smoking in public). As time went on these most dedicated members of the HJ became an important source of auxiliary manpower for the Police. They could be depended upon to act as informants (in many cases even against their own families); and there are even said to have been occasions when the older members provided volunteers for firing squads.

A further auxiliary force, created in 1942, was the Stadtwacht. These members of the SA-Wehrmannschaft provided a direct equivalent to the Landwacht (see below) created for the rural areas, but assisted the Police in large cities. Eventually, virtually every German not in the armed forces or emergency services was made liable for periodic duty in the Stadtwacht or Landwacht. Behind these organizations lay two reserves, one composed of men who would cover initial call-ups for those in the other, whose essential duties exempted them from service in anything but dire emergency. Both Landwacht and Stadtwacht wore a white armband with the name of their organization printed in black letters.

For their security role some Police units had been issued with a limited number of light armoured vehicles since well before the outbreak of war. During the wartime years they received many more for their rear-area security duties outside Germany – usually obsolescent captured types like this French Panhard 178 armoured car, photographed somewhere on the Eastern Front. Note the white Police national emblem painted on the turret; the commander appears to wear a motorcyclist's rubberized coat, and possibly a black Panzer field cap, though the contrasts make it hard to be sure.

Schutzpolizei der Gemeinden

These so-called 'Municipal Police' were effectively a half-way measure between the Gendarmerie, which controlled rural areas with lower population density, and the regular Schupo in densely populated areas. It was intended to extend the responsibility of the Gendarmerie to areas of up to 5,000 inhabitants, which would have reduced the size of the Schupo der Gemeinden even further, but this process had barely started before the war ended. It is estimated that over 1,300 'municipalities' existed which were too large to be controlled by the Gendarmerie but too small for the Schutzpolizei des Reiches.

In such areas, although the true control of Schupo der Gemeinden units lay with the BdO for the area, sited at the Wehrkreis headquarters, they were in practice at the day-to-day disposal of the Bürgermeister of the municipality. Schutzpolizei der Gemeinden in smaller communities were typically commanded by a Hauptmann or Oberleutnant, and were designated as service detachments – Dienstabteilungen. Personnel could move between the Schupo des Reiches and the Schupo der Gemeinden, and the difference between the two, apart from the size of the units and their equipment levels, was predominantly administrative.

Schupo uniforms and insignia
Headgear
The normal service dress headgear for the *Schutzpolizist* was a shako with a stiff fibre body covered in grey-green cloth (greener than the Army

A member of the Schutzpolizei der Gemeinden in service dress with shako. The pale cord edging of his collar patches shows clearly against the dark brown collar, and the wine-red sleeve eagle of the Municipal branch against the pale grey-green tunic. It has no district name above – these were ordered removed from Gemeinde Polizei insignia in late 1941. (Josef Charita)

The Police national emblem in white metal, as displayed on the peaked service caps. The first pattern (left) was smaller and featured an unwreathed swastika; it was replaced with the definitive pattern well before the war.

feldgrau), with black lacquered front and rear peaks (visors) and a flat black lacquered crown; on either side of the body were two mesh ventilation holes, and a black leather chin strap was fitted. The insignia were a large aluminium alloy Police-pattern wreathed eagle national emblem, below an elongated oval cockade in the national colours. Officers wore metal chin scales in place of the leather chin strap, and a cockade embroidered in metallic thread. General officers wore gilt rather than silvered metal fittings. For parade dress, a long black horsehair plume was worn with the shako (later changed to white for officers).

Undress headgear was a peaked (visored) service cap – *Schirmmütze* – with a grey-green crown and a dark brown band. The crown seam and both edges of the band were piped in the appropriate *Truppenfarbe*. The cap had a black lacquered peak; enlisted men and NCOs wore a black leather chin strap and officers silver chin cords. Insignia were a silver-coloured metal Police national emblem on the band, below a circular metal cockade in the national colours on the front of the crown. For general officers the cap piping, chin cords and national emblem were in gilt rather than silver finish.

A field cap – *Feldmütze* or sidecap – in grey-green wool normally featured bright police-green piping along both top crests and down the front of the crown (moved in 1942 to the edge of the flap). It bore a machine-woven version of the Police national emblem in silver-grey on black, but no national cockade. Officers' caps – alone – resembled the M1938 type for Army officers, with silver braid piping to the crown and front of the flap. Insignia for officers were machine-woven in silver thread on black.

Predating the M1943 *Einheitsfeldmütze* of the Wehrmacht, a cloth-visored field cap was introduced for the Police in 1942. It was manufactured in both one- and two-button types, and had silver crown piping for officers (and sometimes *Truppenfarbe* piping for other ranks). Metal insignia were often attached, but special machine-woven one-piece insignia were produced, with the national cockade above the Police national emblem on a grey-green backing.

The full range of steel helmet styles as used in the Wehrmacht and paramilitary units were also issued to the Police. Police helmets featured a shield decal on the left-hand side with a silver Police national emblem on black, and on the right a red shield with white disc and black swastika. Police motorcyclists were issued a special leather crash-helmet, with a reinforced padded band around the lower edge of the crown and a leather visor; a large metal Police national emblem was worn on the front.

Service tunics

The standard *Waffenrock* was cut from grey-green wool, with contrasting dark brown collar and cuff facings. The tunic had two pleated patch breast pockets and two unpleated skirt pockets, all with three-point flaps fastened with single aluminium buttons. The collar, cuffs, front edge and rear skirt panels of the tunic were piped in *Truppenfarbe*. Each cuff had two aluminium buttons sewn one above the other at the rear edge; the front of the tunic was fastened with a single row of eight buttons; and the rear featured two buttons at waist level and one at the base of each *Truppenfarbe*-piped skirt panel (false pocket). As described above under 'Police Insignia', a machine-embroidered Police national emblem was worn on the left sleeve, and mirror-image *Litzen* on the collar; specific branches were identified by *Truppenfarbe* distinctions (see list above), and specific ranks by the shoulder straps. The service tunic was normally worn with matching breeches and black leather jackboots (of a higher quality than the normal Wehrmacht marching boots). For walking-out dress straight grey-green trousers, piped with *Truppenfarbe* at the outseams, were worn loose over black shoes.

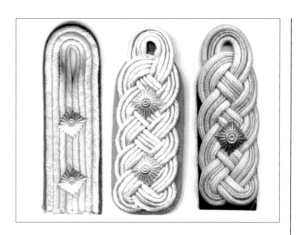

Coats

For cold weather a grey-green double-breasted greatcoat was issued, fastened with two rows of six buttons. This had a cloth rear half-belt with two buttons, and a rear skirt vent from waist to hem. The collar alone was faced with dark brown and piped with *Truppenfarbe*. No collar patches or sleeve eagle were worn. General officers wore gilt buttons. A raincoat was also produced in lightweight waterproof material, to an almost identical pattern to the greatcoat.

Field service tunics

In 1943 an Army-style field service tunic – *Feldbluse* – was produced, as more suitable for front line wear. This was single-breasted, all in grey-green or *feldgrau* wool without collar or cuff facings, and fastened with six buttons painted field-grey. Cuffs were conventional, split up the rear with hidden button fastening. Insignia for enlisted ranks on this tunic tended to be machine-woven artificial silk *Litzen* applied directly to the collar rather than to a coloured backing patch. Officers normally wore the same hand-embroidered insignia as on their service dress tunics. The field service tunic was usually worn with long field-grey wool trousers and marching boots, or ankle boots and canvas gaiters.

Camouflage uniforms

In 1944 a special camouflage field uniform was manufactured for Police troops. This was almost identical to the so-called 'dot-' or 'pea-pattern' field uniform widely used by the Waffen-SS from that year. The non-reversible jacket and trousers were cut in the same lightweight cotton drill material, the jacket with four patch pockets and fastened with six buttons; but a minor peculiarity of the Police issue seems to have been that the breast pockets had box pleats.

Armoured vehicle uniforms

Police units issued with armoured vehicles were authorized to wear the special black clothing for armoured personnel. Similar in cut to the black Panzer uniform used by the Army, its jacket featured bright police-green piping to the collar. Regular Police collar *Litzen* and shoulder straps were attached; but on this jacket the Police sleeve eagle was worked in green on a black base, with a white swastika for contrast. Normal Panzer-issue black trousers were worn, and a version of the black visored field cap was also produced bearing Police insignia.

Accoutrements

Enlisted men wore a black leather belt with both the service dress and field service tunics. The rectangular silver-coloured buckle resembled that of the Army, but in place of the national emblem the wreath and

Police officers' shoulder straps were of identical design to those of the military: (left & centre) Hauptmann and Oberst, silver cord and gilt pips on *Truppenfarbe* underlay; (right) Generalmajor, gold cords with thinner silver cord between, silver pips. Police straps usually have bright aluminium cords, though the wartime matt finish may also be encountered. So may junior officers' straps with an intermediate layer of brown between the cord and the main coloured underlay; these indicate the wartime-only ranks of Revier-Leutnant to Revier-Hauptmann, to differentiate them from career officers.

The hilt of a Police dress bayonet, with eagle-head pommel, staghorn grips with Police eagle, and oak leaf decoration to the quillon. In this case the eagle's eye is a simple engraved circle rather than the spring release catch, showing that this bayonet lacks the catch and slot for attachment to a rifle muzzle. The bayonet was available in different blade lengths: the official issue was 33cm (13in), but private-purchase pieces had 25cm (9.9in) blades.

motto 'Gott Mit Uns' surrounded a large 'mobile' swastika. For parade dress, a white leather waist belt was worn, and a white leather pouch belt over the left shoulder with a black leather pouch displaying a white metal Police eagle on the flap.

Officers normally wore a simple black leather belt with double-claw frame buckle, but on formal occasions added a cross strap from the right shoulder to the left hip; a round silver-coloured clasp bearing the swastika was sometimes seen on the black belt. This clasp was always worn on the full dress belt, which was of aluminium brocade shot with a red line between two black lines; a matching pouch belt was added for parade order.

Sidearms

The standard sidearm for policemen under the rank equivalent of warrant officer was the bayonet. A range of styles had in common a stag-horn grip, oak leaf decoration to the quillon, and a pommel representing an eagle's head – the press-button bayonet release catch suggested the eagle's eye. In some cases the bayonet could actually be fitted to a rifle, in others it lacked the necessary slot and spring and was purely decorative. On the grip was fixed a small alloy Police national emblem. The black leather scabbard had a metal throat and chape and was suspended from a black leather frog. The bayonet ceased to be manufactured in 1941. Thereafter the standard Wehrmacht bayonet tended to be used; and after 1943 the bayonet was replaced by the pistol as the standard sidearm for all but ceremonial occasions.

Police officers and warrant officers were authorized to carry a sword from 21 June 1936. This long, straight-bladed 'Degen' had a D-shaped knucklebow; a button-shaped pommel; a grip of ribbed black wood with silver wire in the grooves, displaying a silvered Police national emblem; and an ornate collar with oak leaf decoration. The scabbard was finished in black enamel paint, with a silvered chape and locket, the latter in an interlaced design. It hung from a single ring and suspension strap. A simpler version was authorized for other NCOs, without the wire wrap to the grip or the silvered chape. The full dress fist straps of bayonets and swords were all of aluminium brocade shot with red-between-black lines, with a plain braid knot.

GENDARMERIE

The Gendarmerie may be defined as the rural Police, maintaining law and order in countryside areas, villages or small towns. Initially these were defined as communities with fewer than 2,000 inhabitants; this was later increased to 5,000, but progress in expanding the Gendarmerie was relatively slow, and most areas with over 2,000 inhabitants remained under the control of the Schutzpolizei. The Gendarme often operated from his own home, and was not far removed in many respects from the typical British 'village bobby' of the day. He was expected not only to enforce the law but to advise the local community on all matters involving officialdom.

The basic unit was in fact the lone officer, known as the Gendarmerie Einzelpost – literally, 'a post filled by an individual'. In larger villages a few policemen might operate under the control of a Wachtmeister or

Oberwachtmeister from a small office. A number of such small posts came under a Gendarmerie Gruppenpost with a senior NCO in administrative control, but he would not interfere with day-to-day matters. Within a geographical district such small posts answered to a Gendarmeriekreisführer or District Police Leader, usually a Leutnant or Oberleutnant in overall charge of perhaps 40 men. In a particularly large district the Gendarmeriekreis might be subdivided into Gendarmerieabteilungen (Police Detachments) each with around 20 men.

The next largest unit was the Gendarmeriehauptmannschaft, with a Hauptmann or Major in control of several Gendarmeriekreise, usually with around 140–150 men. This commander was in turn responsible to the Kommandeur der Gendarmerie for the region. That officer was based at the headquarters of the Befehlshaber der Orpo at the military district headquarters for the region. Final authority lay with the Generalinspekteur der Gendarmerie, within the Hauptampt Orpo in the Ministry of the Interior.

From 1941, in the more remote mountainous regions (generally above 1,500m/ 5,000ft) of Bavaria and Austria, the Gendarmerie were given special training as mountain guides and formed into the 'High Mountain' or Hochgebirgs Gendarmerie.

A junior ranker of the Gendarmerie in service dress. Although the lighter brown of the tunic facings is not evident here, the orange *Truppenfarbe* is visible in the backing to his collar *Litzen*, and (despite the low contrast) can just be made out in a Y-shape of piping on the front of his cap crown. (Josef Charita)

Motorisierte Gendarmerie

This branch was created by Himmler in June 1937 and tasked with the control of traffic on both motorways (Autobahnen) and first-class roads (Landstrassen) – to apprehend stolen vehicles, attend traffic accidents, and so forth. Unlike the regular Gendarmerie, the remit of the Motorized Gendarmerie covered the entire Reich; they could thus pursue a suspect vehicle across the various German 'state lines'. They were housed in barracks and organized along military lines into platoons (Züge) and companies (Kompanien). These units, too, were under the command of the regional Kommandeur der Gendarmerie. The basic unit was the Kompanie, comprising three officers and 108 men, this being subdivided for operational purposes into Züge each of one officer and 36 men; several Kompanien could be assembled into a Gendarmerie Bataillon. After the outbreak of war the Motorized Gendarmerie were also used in the occupied territories to assist the Army's traffic regulators, and to help maintain the security of supply routes. They carried no heavy weapons but were armed with rifles, pistols and machine pistols. On the outbreak of war numbers of former members of the Motorized Gendarmerie were drafted into the Army to help form the military police – Feldgendarmerie.

Landwacht

In rural areas the Gendarmerie could call upon the assistance of the Landwacht, an auxiliary force created in 1942 on the orders of SS-Ogruf Daluege. Part of the perceived need for such a force lay in the presence in rural areas of large numbers of foreign workers (who in 1944 exceeded seven million), some of them paid volunteers, but many conscripted forced labourers and prisoners-of-war who had to be guarded and supervised. The Landwacht were recruited from the SA-Wehrmannschaften – those SA members who had not been called up for military duty but had been given some basic military training. Only cadres were uniformed, as Gendarmerie with a modified Police eagle cap badge incorporating a scroll at the bottom of the wreath; but all personnel were provided with a white armband bearing the legend 'Landwacht' in black block letters low on the brassard. They were armed only with rifles and pistols. National command of the Landwacht was held by SS-Ogruf Friedrich Alpers.

Gendarmerie uniforms and insignia

Headgear

The Gendarmerie shako differed in that the peaks and top were in brown rather than black. Peaked caps were of standard Police pattern, but the band was of a lighter shade of brown, and the piping orange. In the field, a sidecap or peaked field cap was often worn.

Tunics

The basic grey-green uniform for home service was as described above for the Schutzpolizei, but with light rather than dark brown facings, and orange piping and underlays. The Police eagle on the left sleeve was also machine-embroidered in orange on a grey-green base, with the usual black swastika, and initially with the district name embroidered above; officers' eagles were hand-embroidered in silver wire, and lacked the district name. The tunic was worn with either breeches and brown jackboots, or long straight-legged trousers and shoes. The Hochgebirgs Gendarmerie wore mountain trousers and short mountain boots.

Gendarmerie operating outside Germany would eventually receive a field blouse based on the M1943 Army style, in field-grey wool without collar and cuff facings. The sleeve eagle was displayed but lacked any district name. Lightweight summer tunics were also used.

Insignia

Apart from the orange branch colour, Gendarmerie insignia were identical to those used by the Schutzpolizei; but a special cuffband was produced for the motorized branch, and worn on the lower left sleeve just above the cuff. Made from mid-brown wool, it bore the silver-grey title *'Motorisierte Gendarmerie'* in Gothic script; this was machine-embroidered for enlisted ranks and

Two mountain policemen of the Hochgebirgs Gendarmerie. The normal headgear for this branch was a short-peaked cap based on the *Birgmütze* of the mountain troops. Both men display the full-size white metal cap insignia; and the NCO on the right wears the Army-issue padded, reversible grey/white hooded winter overjacket and trousers. (Josef Charita)

hand-embroidered in silver wire for officers, whose bands also had edging in silver 'Russia braid' (a piping with a central seam giving a doubled appearance). A further cuffband in the same colours and style was produced for Gendarmerie personnel working under the control of the Army outside Germany in the occupied territories; this bore the Gothic script title *'Deutsche Wehrmacht'*.

Accoutrements and sidearms

Gendarmerie wore brown leather belts and boots, otherwise identical to those for the Schutzpolizei. Gendarmerie officers and warrant officers used the same sword, and junior ranks the same bayonet as the Schupo, but with brown rather than black scabbards.

Kolonialpolizei

Before the end of World War I, Germany had maintained a number of overseas colonies – in South-West Africa, Cameroon, and at Kiautschau [*sic*], China. In 1936 the Police of three German cities were given the honour of maintaining the traditions of the former Colonial Police: Bremen (SW Africa), Kiel (Cameroon), and Hamburg (Kiautschau). A special cloth tradition badge was worn on the lower left sleeve: a white heater shield with a narrow black cross, and a red upper left canton bearing the five white stars of the 'Southern Cross' constellation. When German forces entered North Africa in 1941, Himmler founded the Kolonialpolizei, tasked with preparing for the employment of the Orpo in future German colonies. It is believed that a small number of Kolonialpolizei may have been employed in North Africa in 1942–43.

Wasserschutzpolizei

The forerunner of the Wasserschutzpolizei (WSP), the Reichswasserschutz, was tasked with the protection of life and property, and the prevention of crimes such as smuggling and unauthorized fishing, on Germany's inland waterways. In 1936, as the Wasserschutzpolizei, it was given its own distinctive naval-style uniform; and in 1937 the WSP officially took responsibility for all Police matters relating to maritime traffic, replacing smaller organizations such as the Schiffahrtspolizei and Hafenpolizei.

On the outbreak of war the Wasserschutzpolizei provided the manpower for the Marineküstenpolizei (MKP), which would perform similar duties in occupied territories; the first MKP units were set up in occupied Denmark in 1940, staffed by former members of the Berlin WSP. These Police personnel then came under the direct control of the Kriegsmarine, although for some time they continued to wear WSP uniforms and insignia. While the WSP covered the inland waterways, the MKP was responsible for securing coastlines and large harbours, and maintaining discipline in naval ports. The WSP also maintained offices or Dienststelle in those occupied areas with inland waterways; one was established in Rotterdam, and others in Poland, Russia, Finland and Serbia.

The organization of the WSP seems to have been extremely flexible. Basic patrols (Wachen) could consist of one or two policemen on foot or bicycle, to patrol the paths bordering canals and riverbanks. In areas of heavier traffic they could use small motor boats, and in some cases might use larger launches

An NCO of the Wasserschutz-polizei wearing that organization's dark blue naval-style uniform – see Plate C3. The peaked *Schirmmütze* is the earlier style with a wire-stiffened crown; it bears a gilt national emblem, and for this rank a black chin strap. Note the single yellow braid cuff ring and yellow sleeve eagle. (Josef Charita)

An Obermeister of the Wasserschutzpolizei, whose senior warrant officer rank entitles him to officer-style gilt cords on his later, unstiffened naval cap. (Josef Charita)

to patrol areas of coastline. WSP squads operated from local stations (Stationen), in turn responsible to precincts (Revier Zweigstellen). The area, district or precinct command was the Revier, under an Oberleutnant or Hauptmann, answerable in turn to a sector (Abschnitt) command, typically under a Major. A group of such sector commands was controlled by a Kommando, usually headed by an Oberstleutnant or Oberst.

Like the land services, the Wasserschutzpolizei could call for assistance from auxiliaries; the NSKK operated its own marine section, the NSKK-Motorbooteinheiten. In some large ports the Allgemeine-SS also provided harbour security units (SS-Hafensicherungstruppen) to assist the Police.

WSP uniforms and insignia

A naval-style peaked cap was worn by WSP personnel, in midnight-blue with a black band, and without piping. The peak (visor) was black; a black leather chin strap was worn by junior ranks and gilt chin cords by officers and warrant officers. The usual national cockade was displayed on the front of the crown, and a gilt metal Police eagle on the band. A sidecap might also be worn; similar to the midnight-blue boarding cap of the Kriegsmarine, it bore a machine-woven Police eagle in yellow on black on the front of the flap, below a national cockade on the crown.

A midnight-blue double-breasted 'reefer' jacket was worn with matching straight trousers (dark blue breeches and high boots were less commonly used), a white shirt and black tie. The jacket had two rows of four gilt buttons. The Police sleeve eagle was in bright yellow embroidery (gold for officers) on dark blue. Shoulder straps of Polizei pattern had, for enlisted ranks, bright yellow central cords and silver outer cords flecked with yellow chevrons, all on a bright yellow underlay. Senior NCOs and warrant officers wore single and double rings of bright yellow braid around both sleeves at cuff level.

The uniform worn by the MKP were eventually replaced with Kriegsmarine issue items, for a transitional period with full Polizei insignia; rank insignia were later replaced with regular Kriegsmarine patterns. There was a narrow midnight-blue left cuffband with yellow edges and 'Marine-Küstenpolizei' in Gothic script. Belts were not worn over the reefer jacket in service dress; in other uniform orders, the buckles of the black leather belts were identical to the Schupo patterns but in gilt rather than silver finish.

Wasserschutzpolizei officers and warrant officers were also authorized their own dress dagger for a limited period; introduced in 1938, it was based on that of the Kriegsmarine. However, the white grip of the naval dagger was replaced with dark blue leather with gilt wire wrap, and fitted with a gilt metal Police emblem. In place of the eagle-and-swastika naval pommel it featured a flaming ball pommel. The dagger was withdrawn in April 1939, after which date it was to be replaced with the regular Police sword.

FEUERSCHUTZPOLIZEI

Before the advent of the Nazi regime, Germany had a two-tier fire brigade system: larger towns and cities had full-time fire-fighters, and rural areas part-time volunteers. In January 1934 the Nazis subordinated all fire-fighting services to the control of the Ordnungspolizei. Interestingly, after the campaign against Poland, Police officials interviewed Polish fire brigade personnel to ascertain how they had dealt with the Luftwaffe's bombing campaign. The result was a decision in late 1939 to form a number of Feuerschutzpolizei regiments. All full-time fire- fighting services in the larger towns were to be transferred to the Feuerschutzpolizei, while the rural part-time volunteer brigades – Feuerwehren – were to be retained. The regiments formed were as follows:

A group of NCOs of the pre-1938 Feuerlöschpolizei illustrate the inconsistency seen during the interim period when both old- and new-style uniforms were being worn. Most wear the old dark blue uniform with carmine distinctions, with the addition of Police cap badges and sleeve eagles. Only the man sitting in the centre of the front row seems to have the full set of new-style insignia. (Josef Charita)

Feuerschutzpolizei Regiment 1 Based in Saxony, elements of the regiment also served in the occupied Netherlands and France, especially around the ports of Le Havre, Lorient, Brest and St Nazaire. A detachment also served on the Eastern Front, where they helped provide protection to the Ploesti oilfields in Romania.

Feuerschutzpolizei Regiment 2 Based in Hanover.

Feuerschutzpolizei Regiment 3 Based in East Prussia, and also served in occupied Poland.

Feuerschutzpolizei Regiment 4 Based in the occupied Ukraine.

Feuerschutzpolizei Regiment 5 Based in occupied Czechoslovakia.

Feuerschutzpolizei Regiment 6 Based in the occupied Netherlands.

At a lower level, as one might expect, the Feuerschutzpolizei were at the disposal of the local civil authorities under the Bürgermeister, who would act in co-ordination with the Polizeipräsident. The costs of operating the Feuerschutzpolizei were borne by the local community they served. Locally, the Feuerschutzpolizei were controlled by the Kommandeur der Feuerschutzpolizei, who would oversee a number of Abschnittskommandos or sector commands, which in turn were subdivided into detachments or Feuerwachen. The smallest single unit was the platoon or Feuerlöschzug, usually comprising two or three fire engines and ten to 12 firemen. Each Feuerwache would comprise several such Feuerloschzüge, the number being determined by the size of town, the fire risk level (e.g. the number of factories, etc), but one Feuerwache would cover the same area as several police precincts.

The 'police' aspect of the Feuerschutzpolizei is explained by the fact that when necessary they could be called upon to take on the tasks of the Gendarmerie or Schutzpolizei if these were unavailable, and that they had full police powers. Thus a member of the Feuerschutzpolizei could, for example, arrest any suspects found at the scene of a suspicious fire. In the early stages of the campaign in the West, Feuerschutzpolizei units followed the armed forces into enemy territory to help save any installations fired by the retreating Allies.

At the height of the Allied bombing offensive it has been estimated that as many as 2 million people served in the Feuerschutzpolizei and Freiwilligen Feuerwehr. As the war dragged on the need for front-line troops saw the ranks of the Feuerschutzpolizei being filled by increasing numbers of eastern 'volunteers' from Poland and the Ukraine. As the Third Reich crumbled a number of Feuerschutzpolizei found themselves in combat situations, thrown into desperate attempts to defend their cities against the enemy.

Generalmajor Walter Goldbach, commander of the Berlin Feuerschutzpolizei, realizing that Germany's final defeat was imminent, had accumulated stocks of fuel; and on 22 April 1945, just before Berlin was finally cut off, he sent his units westwards to safety in Schleswig Holstein, where they surrendered to the British. Four days later Goldbach paid for his devotion to his men; he was shot by the Schupo during his arrest for treason and, though critically injured, he was dragged from his hospital bed and executed just days before the war ended.

FSP uniforms and insignia

Headgear

A peaked cap was issued, in dark blue with a black band, piped in carmine at the crown seam and both edges of the band, and bearing conventional Police insignia. On fire-fighting duty a steel helmet was worn. This generally resembled the Wehrmacht pattern, but was of thinner metal, with two circles of ventilation holes in each side. It had sharply squared-off corners to the brim above the ears in place of the M935 Wehrmacht helmet's smooth curve; and it was made both with (for parade) and without a bright aluminium comb to the top of the skull, contrasting with the black paint finish. Regular Police decals were applied to the sides. It could be fitted with a protective leather neckflap under the side and rear brim.

Tunics

The Feuerschutzpolizei initially wore a dark blue, single-breasted, four-pocket tunic, with eight aluminium front buttons, and carmine piping to the collar, cuff tops, front edge and rear skirt panels. It bore Police-pattern collar patches and shoulder straps worked on carmine underlay. Matching trousers had carmine piping to the outseams.

In 1938 regular grey-green Police uniforms were authorized. These initially featured black collar and cuff facings, and the distinctive carmine piping of this branch; but from 1942 the black facings were changed to Police dark brown. The peaked cap changed to grey-green with a black, later dark brown band with carmine piping. The left sleeves of both tunics displayed the Police national eagle emblem in carmine thread, with

An NCO of the Feuerschutz-polizei gives instruction to a group of Hitler Youth auxiliaries – note their broad fire-fighting belts with a *karabiner* spring hook for a running rope. The instructor displays a district name above the Police national emblem on his left sleeve; he also gives a good side view of the thin, black-painted helmet with its sharply angled break between the front peak and side brim. It is fitted with Y-shaped chin straps for greater security. (Josef Charita)

the district name embroidered above in an arc shape; officers wore silver eagles without the district names.

Accoutrements

The conventional black leather belts with Police buckles were worn by the appropriate ranks with service dress; but a distinctive fire-fighting belt was also worn. This was very broad, with a deep two-claw frame buckle and a wide leather keep; mounted on the left front was a large, bright steel 'karabiner' or spring hook, into which a running rope could be pressed with one hand. A hatchet was worn from this belt on the left hip, haft down, with the head enclosed in a black leather case hanging on a strap.

From 1936, officers and warrant officers were authorized to wear the regular Police sword. Junior ranks were authorized a dress bayonet based on the standard military pattern, but lacking a fixing slot and with an S-shaped quillon. The metal fittings were nickel-plated, and the grip in chequered black Bakelite. Blade length was 35cm (13.75in) for NCOs and 40cm (15.75in) for junior enlisted ranks; saw-backed blades could also be provided at extra cost – all of these dress sidearms were privately purchased rather than official issue.

Feuerwehren

Although this branch should really be considered an auxiliary force, it is dealt with here for the sake of simplicity. As already noted, the Feuerwehr consisted of those part-time volunteer firemen who served rural communities, but also included some other, smaller organizations:

Freiwillige Feuerwehr The local part-time volunteer fire brigades in rural communities; after the creation of the Feuerschutzpolizei, these were officially classed as Technische Hilfspolizei (Technical Auxiliary Police). Each village or district was obliged by law to create such a fire service. Although civilian volunteers, the members came under the direct control of the Ordnungspolizei.

Pflichtfeuerwehr With wartime demands on manpower, there were often occasions when there were insufficient volunteers to create a fire brigade. In such cases the authorities were entitled to draft suitable individuals for compulsory service. All German males between 17 and 65 were liable for call-up to serve in the Feuerwehr.

Werkfeuerwehren These were organized by the management of individual factories and manned by employees of the firm. The decision as to whether a Werkfeuerwehr was to be created was a matter for higher authorities. Minimum manpower requirement for a Werkfeuerwehr was 18 men and one power-driven pump unit.

HJ-Feuerwehrscharen The Hitler Jugend also contributed volunteer auxiliary firemen. Each HJ-Feuerwehrschar consisted of around 45 to 50 youths divided into three fire-fighting squads or Kameradschaften, trained and equipped by the local Feuerwehr and at the disposal of the local fire chief.

The costs of all of these Feuerwehren were met by the local community. Feuerwehren within an area were under the control of a Bezirksführer appointed by the local Police President. His area of

Female auxiliaries serving with the Feuerschutzpolizei being fitted with the black-painted FSP steel helmet, complete with its leather neck flap; this photo clearly shows the silver-grey-on-black Police decal on the left side and the red, white and black Party decal on the right. The women wear thick protective clothing with fly fronts and open patch pockets, in an unidentified shade probably of either grey or blue; on the left sleeve a district name and Police national emblem are sharply visible, apparently in white on a dark patch. (Josef Charita)

command would then be divided into several Kreise or districts each under a Kreisführer; subordinate to the Kreisführer might be several Unterkreisführer, with each individual Feuerwehr unit commanded by a Wehrführer. In the case of Pflichtfeuerwehren, such units came under the control of the nearest Feuerschutzpolizei commander.

The Feuerwehr wore the same dark blue uniform as the Feuerschutzpolizei, but with their own collar patch and shoulder strap insignia.

LUFTSCHUTZPOLIZEI
The responsibility for air raid precautions (hereafter in this text, ARP) and assistance initially lay with the pre-war Reichsluftschutzbund (RLB), a semi-official Party-sponsored organization. This was later taken over by the Air Ministry, and in each Luftgau or 'air district' of Germany an RLB Gruppenführer was appointed to control ARP matters in that area. The RLB were designated as auxiliary policemen when carrying out their duties; a large proportion of the members were part-time volunteers.

Working with the RLB were the RLB Warndienst (Air Raid Warning Service – see below); and the Sicherheits und Hilfsdienst (SHD), which was a mobile Civil Defence force of fire-fighters, decontamination squads, repair, demolition, medical and veterinary units. SHD men were conscripts who were employed full time and stationed in barracks, but were allowed to sleep out in rotation, and were exempt from military conscription while serving. Mobile SHD units were allocated to just over 100 cities in Germany – those considered most likely to suffer air attacks.

With the onset of the major Allied bombing campaign against Germany it quickly became clear that the existing ARP structures were unable to cope; and in March 1942, Himmler instituted a new organization, the Luftschutzpolizei, under his own direct command. Personnel of the former motorized units of the SHD were absorbed into the Luftwaffe as Luftschutz Abteilungen, continuing to carry out principally fire-fighting, demolition and rescue duties but under the control of the Luftwaffe rather than the Polizei. All other SHD personnel were absorbed into the new Luftschutzpolizei. The Luftschutzpolizei included both full-time regular personnel and part-time auxiliaries; the full-time elements comprised the following specialist units:

Feuer- und Entgiftungsdienst Regular fire-fighting and decontamination units, which were trained by the Feuerschutzpolizei.

Instandsetzungsdienst Responsible for emergency demolition of unsafe buildings and repairs to those that could be saved.

Fachtruppe Technical specialists to deal with damaged gas mains, water mains, power cables, sewers, etc.

Two members of the Feuerschutzpolizei, wearing the grey-green uniform of the 1938 regulation, pose with a fire brigade officer in the old blue uniform, and a unit from one of the volunteer Feuerwehren in the provinces. These part-time fire-fighters have been issued military M1935 helmets, and two-piece protective clothing with exposed buttons and two patch pockets with pointed flaps. Apart from helmet decals no insignia are visible; but note the broad belts with spring hooks, and the cased hatchets hanging low on the left hip. (Josef Charita)

(continued on page 33)

PRE-UNIFICATION POLICE, 1933–34
1: SA-Scharführer, SA-Feldjägerkorps
2: Oberwachtmeister, Bavarian Landespolizei
3: Jäger, Landespolizeigruppe General Göring

1

2

3

A

UNIFIED NATIONAL POLICE, 1937–40
1: Oberstleutnant, Schutzpolizei, c.1938 (Paradeanzug)
2: Leutnant standard-bearer, Schupo; Berlin, 1937
3: Generalmajor, Ordnungspolizei,
   c.1940 (Meldeanzug)

B

1: Oberleutnant, Verwaltungspolizei, c.1941–43 (Ausgehanzug)
2: Major, Schupo, c.1941–43 (Dienstanzug)
3: Meister, Wasserschutzpolizei, 1939 (Ausgehanzug)

1

2

3

MUNICIPAL POLICE & GENDARMERIE, 1941–43
1: Hauptwachtmeister, Schupo der Gemeinden
2: Oberleutnant, Motorisierte Gendarmerie
3: Wachtmeister, Hochgebirgs Gendarmerie

D

FIRE & AIR PROTECTION POLICE
1: Wachtmeister, Feuerschutzpolizei, c. 1938
2: Hauptmann, Feuerschutzpolizei, 1938–42
3: Zugführer, Luftschutzpolizei, 1942–45

1

2

3

E

TN, RAILWAY & FACTORY POLICE
1: TN-Bereitschaftsführer, Technische Nothilfe, 1942
2: Bzp-Oberabteilungsführer, Bahnschutzpolizei
3: Werkschutzpolizist, c.1944

F

PRISONS, POSTAL PROTECTION & POLICE GENERAL

1: Strafanstaltbeamte, prison service, 1940
2: Abteilungshauptführer, Postschutz, pre-1942
3: Generaloberst der Ordnungspolizei, 1944

1

3

2

G

ARMED POLICE, 1943–45
1: Wachtmeister, Schutzpolizei, c.1943
2: Meister, Schutzpolizei armoured troops, 1944
3: Oberwachtmeister, Schutzpolizei, 1945

H

Luftschutzsanitätsdienst First aid branch.
Luftschutzveterinärdienst Veterinary branch.

As an auxiliary force, the Luftschutzpolizei were subordinate to the Ordnungspolizei; they took their instructions from the regular Police, and personnel did not have powers of arrest. As wartime pressure on manpower increased, women were also recruited into the Luftschutzpolizei to release men for military service.

Uniforms and insignia

The former SHD kept their original Luftwaffe-style uniforms, initially with their own distinctive insignia, including dark green collar patches of Luftwaffe shape bearing the letters 'SHD' in silver-grey Gothic script; enlisted ranks' patches had green-and-white twist edging, officers' patches plain silver cord; officers also wore Luftwaffe-style silver cord piping around the top half of the open tunic collar. Shoulder straps were narrow; for enlisted ranks they were of dark emerald-green, with for NCOs a narrow silver cord inset from the edges, and aluminium pips where appropriate; for officers they were of silver cord on green underlay, with a single green cord inset from the edges for junior ranks, and gilt pips.

A special silver RLB badge was worn on the cap crown, above a national cockade on the band; and embroidered, in silver thread on the right breast for officers, and in white on the upper left sleeve for enlisted ranks. This was two spread wings in roughly the style of the Luftwaffe national emblem, with a central wreath and 'Luftschutz' scroll above a swastika.

The different types of unit were identified by oval cloth patches bearing Gothic script characters, worn on the lower left sleeve: F (= *Feuerlösch- und Entgiftungsdienst*) – white, on red patch with green edging; I (= *Instandsetzung*) – white, on brown patch with green edging; G (=*Gasspüren- und Entgiften Ausgebildete*) – black, on yellow patch with green edging, worn by Fachtruppe trained in gas detection; caduceus symbol (= *Sänitätsdienst*) – white, on pale blue patch with green edging; V (=*Veterinärdienst*) – white, on violet patch with green edging. In addition, from December 1941 a green armband was worn on the upper left sleeve, bearing the legend '*Sicherheits-u. /hilfsdienst*' in two lines of yellow Gothic script. This armband also served to indicate the wearer's grade in the organization by means of narrow and wide braid edgings of various types.

The rank titles in the SHD went from SHD-Mann to SHD-Stabsgruppenführer, equivalent to military ranks from Schutze to Stabsfeldwebel; and from SHD-Zugführer to SHD-Abteilungsführer, equivalent to ranks from Leutnant to Oberstleutnant. Police ranks were adopted when the SHD was absorbed into the Luftschutzpolizei, but this was a gradual process.

After their transfer into the Luftschutzpolizei it was intended that these personnel would eventually receive the regular Police grey-green uniform; this change seems never to have been fully implemented, but photos show a gradual change to Police cap, sleeve and collar insignia on the Luftwaffe-style blue-grey uniforms.

From the days of the original RLB a special steel helmet was worn: resembling the military M1935 but with a broader appearance, it was of

A blurred but rare photograph of an officer of the Luftschutz-polizei, wearing the Luftwaffe-style service cap and uniform with Police badges as introduced for the new service after March 1942, when it was created from part of the former Sicherheits und Hilfsdienst – see Plate E3. The collar patches are of Police type, and are on black underlay, as are the narrow silver shoulder cords. (Josef Charita)

Another group of female auxiliaries receive helmets, this time the broad Reichsluftschutz-bund pattern with a raised rib around the base of the skull. These helmets were painted Luftwaffe dark blue-grey, and bore the Luftschutz decal on the front in silver-grey. Yet another type of protective one-piece coveralls can be seen here, apparently in a waterproofed cloth. (Robert Noss)

thin steel, with a raised rib all round the base of the skull and ventilation holes each side. A decal of the Luftschutz winged badge was worn on the front. This helmet remained in use by the Air Protection services throughout the war.

In all the 'hands-on' emergency services, both full- and part-time, personnel were issued for hard physical labour a variety of off-white (undyed) cotton drill jackets and trousers, or baggy overalls in various shades of grey, blue and brown.

* * *

As the Luftschutzpolizei was subordinate to the Orpo, so other, lesser organizations were subordinated to it:

Werkluftschutzdienst Factory air raid services, recruited from factory staff and supervised by local management.

Werkschutzpolizei Also recruited from factory staff, their primary task was prevention of theft or sabotage, but they were often called upon to work alongside the Werkluftschutzdienst. Werkschutz personnel were usually issued military-style uniforms of either dark blue or dull grey, which might have either open or closed collars, and a military-style peaked cap. Insignia varied widely, but usually included the Werkschutz cap and sleeve badges; cuffbands were issued in various colours, with the legend '*Werkschutz*' in block letters. The left sleeve badge was embroidered in silver-grey on a black or grey oval edged with silver-grey cord; it showed a stylized factory over half a cogwheel, between wings, all 'protected' at the left by a tilted shield emblazoned with a black swastika. The aluminium cap badge was a distinctively shaped eagle with the same shield. In some cases a company logo might be worn in the form of collar patches.

It would appear that control of these personnel remained under Göring's Air Ministry and was not transferred to the Ordnungspolizei, as were most other such smaller organizations.

Selbstschutz These were the purely civilian volunteers who acted as fire-watchers, wardens at apartment blocks, etc, and were broadly equivalent to the ARP volunteers found in Britain. Similar volunteers worked in the commercial (as opposed to industrial) sectors, providing wardens for department stores, hotels, theatres and other buildings.

Luftschutzwarndienst Broadly similar to Britain's Observer Corps, their job was to provide early warning of approaching enemy aircraft. They were absorbed by the Luftwaffe in 1942, but civilian auxiliaries, both male and female, still worked alongside their Luftwaffe and Police colleagues.[4] Luftwaffe-style uniforms were worn, initially with the same shoulder straps and collar patches as the SHD, but with the letters 'LSW' on the dark green patches.

TECHNISCHE NOTHILFE

The Technical Emergency Service (TeNo or TN) was composed of technical specialists in a wide range of disciplines which were essential in responding to emergency situations in both peace and war: construction, demolition, maintaining and repairing the means of

4 See MAA 393, *World War II German Women's Auxiliary Services*

power and water supply, land and waterway communications, and so forth. It had been founded in September 1919, when it effectively acted as a strike-breaking force during the political unrest of the first years of the Weimar Republic, to ensure that essential services were maintained. In 1937 it became an auxiliary branch of the Order Police. In 1939 its members were given the right to bear arms.

During wartime, TeNo members were generally above the age for military service (between 45 and 70 years). Although membership was voluntary – at least initially – once accepted a member could not simply leave at will. The basic TeNo unit was the Kompanie, which comprised several specialist sections. Five such companies could be assembled to form a TeNo Abteilung, covering a geographical area; it is believed that about 13 such areas had their own TeNo Abteilungen. In addition, TeNo units operated alongside the Wehrmacht, providing specialist advice and assistance in the occupied territories. Such units were controlled by a TeNo-Einsatzkommando located with the senior Army headquarters in the region.

TeNo uniforms and insignia

Prior to the outbreak of war TeNo personnel wore a midnight-blue uniform consisting of an Army-style field cap (sidecap) or peaked service cap; a four-pocket, open-collar tunic with four aluminium front buttons; a white shirt and black tie; midnight-blue trousers, jackboots or shoes. A matching double-breasted greatcoat had two rows of aluminium front buttons, and displayed collar, shoulder and sleeve insignia.

Insignia were in white or silver (depending on rank) on black. The distinctive piping around enlisted ranks' shoulder straps and collar patches was white with a light black fleck. Officers seem to have worn black-flecked silver edging on collar patches, plain silver piping on caps, and plain black underlay on shoulder straps. Four main 'services' or branches were distinguished by coloured piping on officers' collars of the blue uniform, and the fist straps of dress sidearms: blue (Technical Service, TD); red (Air Protection Service, LD); orange-yellow (Emergency Service, BD); and green (General Service, AD).

From 1940 those personnel attached to the armed forces were issued a plain field-grey Army-style uniform, with a black band and silver piping on the officer's peaked cap; this uniform became increasingly common during the war. From October 1942 a change to Police uniform was ordered, with black facings and sleeve eagle, but this seems to have been only partly achieved.

The service had its own complex rank title sequence, which was revised in 1941 and again in 1943, some rank insignia being changed accordingly; the picture is further confused by the fact that blocks of several ranks wore the same insignia. In 1937–41 black rectangular collar patches with cord twist edging showed the rank on the left patch, and for all ranks below TN-Landesführer the wearer's unit and detachment, by a combination of Roman above Arabic numerals, on the right.

The RLB national emblem, here in woven form for the uniform, but also used as a decal on the Luftschutz helmet worn by personnel of the SHD and Luftschutzpolizei.

The national emblem worn by the Technische Nothilfe as a left sleeve eagle. Machine-embroidered in white or silver on black, it shows the TeNo cogwheel, hammer and 'N' superimposed on the large swastika.

Ranks were identified by a combination of cogwheel and laurel leaf emblems; the three most senior ranks displayed the rank on both patches. Photos dating from 1941–43 show all officer grades with mirror-image rank patches. During 1943 collar patches changed to SS pattern, with rank worn on both collars; TeNo shoulder straps are believed to have been retained.

Junior enlisted ranks' shoulder straps were black, pointed, edged with black-flecked white, and differenced by transverse white or silver-grey bars; NCO-equivalent ranks wore narrow, officer-style straps on black underlay, of silver cord with a single black cord inset from the long edges, and differenced by gilt bars; and officer-equivalents wore similar straps with plain silver cords differenced by gilt cogwheel-and-star pips. Representative examples, 1937–41, are:

TN-Vormann (equivalent to senior private): right hand patch, embroidered 'VII/2'; left hand patch, pressed aluminium cogwheel centred; broad pointed shoulder straps, three narrow silver-grey bars across outer end.

TN-Gefolgschaftsführer (equivalent to Hauptmann): right hand patch, silver embroidered 'II'; left hand patch, cogwheel above embroidered symmetrical double spray of laurels; narrow rounded shoulder straps, silver cord on black underlay, two gilt pips.

A national emblem of special TeNo pattern was worn on the upper left sleeve of the blue and field-grey uniforms (see photograph). White-on-black trade badges were also seen, in the form of letters or symbols surrounded by the TeNo cogwheel.

A cuffband, bearing the legend '*Technisches Nothilfe*' in silver or silver-grey Gothic script on black, between matching edgings, was sometimes worn on the left forearm of the field-grey Army-style uniform. As well as or in place of this, personnel serving with the armed forces wore a yellow brassard on the upper left arm, with the black Gothic legend '*Deutsches Wehrmacht*'.

On the crown of the officer's peaked cap an aluminium badge showed the TeNo national emblem, in this case with the swastika set on a diamond-shaped extension rather than the usual round Wehrmacht wreath. On the band the national cockade was centred in an Army-style embroidered silver wreath, and the usual silver cap cords were worn. A small machine-woven version of the TeNo national emblem was worn on the front of the blue and field-grey sidecaps, in silver-grey on black, above a plain cockade.

In reality, the uniform most often worn when working was a simple undyed herringbone drill fatigue suit, often devoid of insignia.

Sidearms

Junior ranks of the TeNo were issued with a dress 'hewer'. This had a heavy scimitar-style blade, a crossguard bearing the TeNo national emblem, a white grip, and a pommel vaguely in the shape of a stylized eagle's head with a cogwheel as the 'eye'. The metal scabbard was painted black with silvered throat and chape fittings. TeNo officers wore instead a dagger proportioned similarly to those worn by the Army, with a white spirally grooved grip, a crossguard with the TeNo national emblem, and a pommel bearing a large cogwheel.

SPECIAL & AUXILIARY POLICE

The Sonderpolizei comprised a number of organizations that were not integral parts of the Ordnungspolizei, though they might carry out similar duties. These included:

Bahnschutzpolizei

A subordinate organization of the German Railways (Deutsche Reichsbahn), this was effectively the Transport Police force. They could on occasion be called upon to assist the regular Police, in which cases command would transfer from the Reichsbahn to the Orpo, and personnel would temporarily acquire the status of auxiliary policemen. Control of the Bahnschutzpolizei eventually passed from the Reichsbahn to the Ordnungspolizei.

Uniforms and insignia
The Bahnschutzpolizei were issued a pale blue-grey uniform with a dark blue-grey collar. The peaked cap had a dark blue-grey band; enlisted ranks had a black chin strap, officer ranks silver piping and chin cords. The crown badge was an aluminium eagle very similar to that of the Wehrmacht; the band badge, the national cockade centred in a wreath incorporating a winged wheel motif.

The tunic had up to eight aluminium front buttons, four pleated patch pockets and plain cuffs, and was made in both closed- and open-collar styles, in the latter case worn with a white shirt and black tie. A white or silver thread Bahnschutz sleeve eagle, very similar to the style originally used by the SS-Verfügungstruppe, was worn on the upper left arm. From 1941 a range of specialists' and appointment badges, in white or (from Bzp-Abteilungsführer upwards) silver thread on blue-grey discs, were worn on the right forearm.

It had been intended that a uniform in field-grey should be used during wartime, but this was never introduced.

As in other sections of this text, space forbids a complete listing of the rank sequence, which was extraordinarily complex. Ranks ran from Bzp-Anwärter (equivalent to private) to Bzp-Zugführer (Ober-feldwebel), and from Bzp-Oberzugführer (equivalent to Leutnant) to Chef der Bahnschutzpolizei (Generalleutnant). Mirror-image black collar patches were of Army shape for the closed collar and upright shape for the open collar. They displayed the winged wheel motif of the German Railways, with a sequence of rank distinctions in the form of narrow and broad borders and four-point stars, in silver-grey or silver.

Enlisted ranks' shoulder straps were rounded, basically black and roughly resembling Police styles. Junior NCO ranks showed black cords flecked with silver chevrons; senior NCOs, silver outer cords flecked with black chevrons, and differenced by silver pips; all these bore a silver winged wheel and a unit number. Most officer ranks wore Army-style shoulder straps, in silver cord flecked with black chevrons on black underlay, differenced by gilt pips and bearing a gilt winged wheel and unit numbers. Some specific ranks (Bzp-Oberzugführer, Abteilungs-führer & Bezirksführer) wore instead very narrow shoulder cords without backing or metal insignia, straight or interwoven, in silver flecked with black chevrons.

Even protection of the postal service was eventually taken over entirely by the SS, like every other policing function. This interesting 1945 snapshot shows not a German SS auxiliary, but a female soldier of the Red Army posing in a captured field cap and tunic – the unedged black cuffband with the title 'SS-Postchutz' is clearly visible. Note also the SS sleeve eagle; the black collar patches with some kind of pale edging, the right patch blank and the left with an SS-Unterschar-führer's pip; and what seem to be shoulder cords in bold black-and-white twist – they appear too thick to be simply *Waffenfarbe* edging on a cloth strap.

In 1941 a range of cuffbands was introduced, bearing the legend 'Bahnschutzpolizei' in Gothic script; different colours were worn by various sequences of ranks. From junior to senior, these were: silver-grey on black, matching edges; silver on black, matching edges; black on white, black edges; black on silver, darker silver edges; gold on silver, white edges; and (for the national Chief of the service) silver on gold brocade, silver edges.

Representative examples of rank insignia, 1941–45, are as follows:

Bzp-Stellvertreter Gruppenführer (equivalent to Gefreiter): Black collar patches with narrow border and winged wheel in silver-grey; shoulder straps completely faced with black cord flecked with silver chevrons, on black underlay, with silver winged wheel and '23'; black cuffband, silver-grey title and edges.

Bzp-Oberabteilungsführer (equivalent to Hauptmann): Black collar patches with broad doubled border, winged wheel and one star, embroidered in silver; shoulder straps in silver cord flecked with black chevrons, on black underlay, with gilt winged wheel and '5'; aluminium brocade cuffband, darker edges, black title.

Sidearms

Pistols were carried for everyday service. Bahnschutzpolizei officers were authorized to wear a dress dagger similar to that of the Army but with a black grip, a ball pommel embellished with a swastika, and a crossguard featuring the winged wheel emblem.

Two members of the Mines Police (Bergpolizei), uniformed in the black which was the traditional colour of miners' formal costume. Only the cap shows the Police eagle; the white left-arm badge is a crossed hammer and pick in a silver chevron. (Josef Charita)

Postschutz

This small Postal Protection organization was formed in March 1933, originally under the control of the Reichspostministerium and headed by NSKK-Obergruppenführer Dr Ohnesorge. It was responsible for protecting property belonging to the postal, telephone and telegraph services throughout the Reich. In 1942 it was absorbed into the Allgemeine-SS, being retitled the SS-Postschutz.

Uniforms and insignia

Personnel wore a field-grey peaked service cap with a dark green band, piped in the orange distinctive colour of the postal service. Insignia were an aluminium spread-winged eagle on the crown, and on the band the national cockade surrounded by a wreath incorporating a double-ended bundle of three lightning bolts; black chin straps and silver chin cords were worn by enlisted and officer ranks.

The field-grey, Army-style, single-breasted, closed-collar tunic had five aluminium front buttons, dark green collar facing, four pleated patch pockets and plain cuffs. The uniform was completed by field-grey breeches or trousers, and jackboots or shoes; the walking-out trousers had orange piping on the outseams.

Collar patches were of SS shape, mid-green with orange edge piping; rank insignia were of SS pattern, in silver-grey or silver, in mirrored pairs. Enlisted shoulder straps were field-grey, with orange piping and, where appropriate, silver-grey NCO Tresse and silver rank pips; officer straps were of silver cord on orange underlay, with gilt pips.

A national emblem showing a spread-winged eagle and swastika with three double-ended lightning bolts was worn on the upper left sleeve, in white for enlisted and silver for officer ranks. A grey cuffband with the legend '*Postschutz*' in orange Gothic script was also produced, but details of its wear are uncertain.

After its absorption into the Allgemeine-SS, the Postschutz wore silver-grey and silver SS rank insignia on black patches, and a cuffband with the legend '*SS-Postschutz*' in silver-grey on black.

Funkschutz

Another organ of the Reichspostministerium, the Funkschutz provided guards for the transmitting stations of the broadcasting authorities. They were also involved in tracking down illegal transmitters. Details of any special uniform insignia are unknown.

Auxiliary police

The Auxiliary Police included a range of units, usually created from Nazi Party organizations, which could provide specialist assistance to the Ordnungspolizei when required. These included:

NSKK-Verkehrsdienst Traffic control units of the Nazi Party motorized corps.

NSKK-Verkehrserziehungsdienst Driving instruction service (this issued all driving licences).

NSKK-Verkehrshilfsdienst Motorists' aid service.

NSKK-Transportkontrollen des motorisierten Transportes der Kriegswirtschaften NSKK unit for inspection of cargo on wartime motor transport.

SA-Feldpolizei Formed in August 1933, these were SA auxiliaries who assisted the regular Police in maintaining order, especially in large cities, during the early days of the regime. They wore standard SA uniform but with black tops to their kepis and black collar patches, the right-hand patch bearing the Prussian Police star. A duty gorget was worn, with a gilt static swastika at each end, flanking the Police star in the centre, over the issue number.

SA-Feldjäger Formed in late 1933 as the SA's own police force, it was also used to support the regular Police. SA uniform was worn, with a white-topped kepi and white collar patches; see Plate A1 for details. When this unit was disbanded in April 1935 its members were absorbed into the Police, and briefly formed motorized Autobahn patrols; they wore Police uniform but with their former white facing colour – on the cap band and piping; as piping on the collar, tunic front, and the top of

Riding in a Police car with a member of the Prussian Schutzpolizei, 1933/34, this SA-Sturmführer wears the telltale white distinctions of the SA-Feldjägerkorps auxiliaries – see Plate A1. In this case, as a junior officer, he displays black/silver twist piping to the kepi and collar patches. (Josef Charita)

A female Police auxiliary on traffic duty. She wears yet another variation on the heavy coveralls which seem to have been the most common clothing for women auxiliaries on outdoor duties. The Police national emblem appears on both the field cap and the left sleeve. (Josef Charita)

the plain grey cuffs; as backing for the collar patches and shoulder straps, and as the colour of the sleeve eagle. In 1937 their role was taken over by the Motorisierte Gendarmerie.

SS-Industrieschutzmannschaft Industrial safety unit of the SS.

ORDNUNGSPOLIZEI ADMINISTRATIVE BRANCH

The Orpo administrative branch or Verwaltungspolizei was quite separate from the executive branches. It was organized into local administrative departments or Staatliche Polizeiverwaltungen, each comprising five sections:

Wirtschaftsabteilung This section dealt with accounting and bookkeeping, payrolls, pensions and allowances, uniforms, subsistence and accommodation budgets, and related matters.

Passwesen, Ausländerpolizei, Meldewesen, Wehrersatzwesen These four sections dealt with passport regulations, control of foreigners in Germany (issue of residence permits, etc), civil registration regulations, registration of recruits for the armed forces, citizenship, emigration, registration of changes of name and address, and so forth – the whole bureaucratic machinery by which a police state maintains scrutiny and control of every detail of everyday life.

Uniforms These were identical to those of the Schutzpolizei, with the exceptions of light grey piping and collar patch bases and shoulder strap underlay, the latter with a carmine inner underlay.

Female auxiliaries

Unlike the Wehrmacht, whose admission of female auxiliaries was a result of wartime necessity, the Police had always employed women in clerical and communications roles, and to assist their male colleagues when female suspects were arrested or held in custody.

Uniforms Police auxiliaries wore a field cap (sidecap), a single-breasted three-button jacket with an open, notched collar, and a pleated skirt, all in grey-green Police uniform colour. The field cap was of Luftwaffe cut, with the Police national emblem, woven in silver-grey on black, on the front of the flap; no national cockade was worn. Bright green piping on the top crests, or later the edge of the flap, has also been illustrated. The Police national emblem was worn on the upper left sleeve in bright green; alternatively, photos show the small cap version in silver-grey on black worn as a left-cuff badge. Other sources show a grey indoor working dress with a full-length buttoning front closure, two pleated patch breast pockets, buttoned cuffs and an integral cloth belt, also displaying the green sleeve eagle.[5]

Prison officials

Although originally controlled by the Ministry of the Interior, the prison officials – Strafanstaltbeamte – are worth mention here, since they were ultimately absorbed by the Police. The prison system was split into two parallel parts: 'ordinary' prisons for conventional criminals, predating the Nazi regime and administered by civil officials under court supervision; and 'extraordinary' prisons and camps for political prisoners, under the authority of Heydrich's (later Kaltenbrunner's) Sicherheitspolizei and Gestapo.

5 See MAA 393, *World War II German Women's Auxiliary Services*

The *Dienstauszeichnung* for 25 years' service: a gilt cross, on a cornflower-blue ribbon embroidered in golden-yellow with a miniature Police eagle.

The *Bandenkampfabzeichen* or Anti-Partisan War Badge, earned by many policemen serving in the occupied Eastern and Southern territories and awarded in three classes. A rare and desirable piece for collectors, this badge has been extensively counterfeited, sometimes with great skill.

As might be expected of the German system, the ordinary prisons comprised a complex variety of institutions with different designations, staffed by officials of an equally complex sequence of grades. The basic uniform consisted of a peaked service cap, single-breasted tunic and matching breeches all in Police grey-green, worn with black jackboots.

The peaked cap had a dark green band and carmine piping; the insignia were a rather squat gilt national emblem on the crown above a plain cockade on the band, and the dark green chin cords had a gold fleck pattern.

The tunic was normally of closed-collar style, with six gilt front buttons, pleated patch breast pockets and internal skirt pockets. 'Lace and metal' were golden-yellow and gilt, and the collar and cuffs were piped in carmine. Shoulder straps were of Police pattern, on carmine underlay; those of enlisted ranks were of dark green cord flecked with gold, for senior NCOs edged with gold cord flecked with green chevrons and with rank differences in the form of gilt flower-shaped pips. Collar patches were plain dark green, with carmine piping for junior and gold twist piping for senior ranks; all bore an embossed gilt button at the rear end, plus a central horizontal strip of gilt braid for senior ranks. No sleeve eagle was worn.

Accoutrements and sidearms

A black belt was worn with a gilt clasp, of slightly oval shape; the design was a wreath around an old Prussian royal eagle with lightnings in one talon and a broadsword in the other. For ceremonial purposes prison officials were authorized a sabre in Army style, but with an attractive gilt eagle's-head pommel – one of the more impressive of Third Reich period edged weapons.

PERSONAL AWARDS & DOCUMENTS

A series of long-service awards for the Police was introduced in January 1938. Awards were made on the completion of the requisite number of years of good conduct and loyal service, as follows:

8 Years A circular silvered medal 38mm (1.5in) in diameter, bearing the Police national emblem on the obverse, and the number '8' within a wreath on the reverse. Worn on a plain cornflower-blue ribbon.

18 Years A silvered bronze cross c.43mm x 43mm (1.7in), with the Police emblem in an oval wreath overlaying the centre of the obverse. On the reverse centre an oval medallion bears the legend 'Für Treue Dienst in der Polizei' (For Faithful Service in the Police) in Gothic script. Worn on a cornflower-blue ribbon, with the Police emblem embroidered centrally in silver-grey thread.

25 Years A gilt bronze cross of the same dimensions and design as the above. Worn from a cornflower-blue ribbon, with the Police emblem embroidered centrally in golden-yellow thread.

Anti-Partisan War Badge

When serving in war zones, Police personnel were entitled to receive any military decorations for which their deeds qualified them. Thus the War Merit Cross, Iron Cross, Wound Badge, etc, were often awarded to members of the Schutzpolizei and Gendarmerie, especially those

 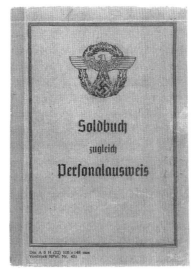

involved in anti-partisan operations in the occupied areas on the Eastern Front. One award specifically intended principally for SS and Police units – although also widely awarded to Wehrmacht personnel – was the Bandenkampfabzeichen (Anti-Partisan War Badge).

Instituted by Himmler on 30 January 1944, the badge consisted of an oval wreath of oak leaves in the centre of which was an ancient sword, with a Germanic sunwheel swastika below the hilt, plunging down through a mythical hydra with five snakes' heads – representing the partisans – into a death's-head at the bottom of the wreath. The award was authorized in three grades: Bronze, for 20 days in action against partisans; Silver, for 50 days; and Gold, for 100 days.

The badge was in pin-back form, and worn on the left breast pocket. Initial production pieces were die-struck with a solid back, but the vast majority of examples encountered are die-cast in zink, with a semi-hollow back.

Personal identification

Police personnel were issued with a Dienstpass, which was roughly equivalent to the military Wehrpass, containing numerous personal details and records of training, postings, awards, etc. Unlike military Wehrpässe, however, these Dienstpasse rarely contain a photograph of the holder.

As a more formal identity document, the policeman received a Soldbuch, which was the direct equivalent of that issued to members of the armed forces. This paybook normally included a photograph of the bearer on the inside front cover, as well as personal details, a record of promotions, pay grades, kit issues, medical treatment, and many other minutiae of his service.

Both documents carried the Police national emblem on the cover until 1942; after that year the Soldbuch with the Police eagle was gradually replaced with a type bearing the SS runes.

A further form of ID carried by some Police officials was the warrant disc. This was an oval metal tag carried on a chain; the obverse showed the Police national emblem, and the reverse the Police organization to which the bearer belonged and his ID number. The best known of these tags were, of course, those issued to members of the Gestapo and the Kripo; these bore the legend 'Geheime Staatspolizei' or 'Staatliche Kriminalpolizei' as appropriate, above the serial number. Rarer than these in terms of numbers was the disc carried by members of the Gemeinde Polizei.

The *Polizei Dienstpass,* the Police equivalent of the military *Wehrpass* (left); and a pre-1943 example of the more detailed paybook or *Soldbuch* (right) – after that date the cover bore the SS runes in place of the Police national emblem. The cover of the *Dienstpass* clearly states that it is not intended as a formal ID document or *Ausweiss;* unlike the *Soldbuch,* it contained no photograph of the bearer.

PLATE COMMENTARIES

A: PRE-UNIFICATION POLICE, 1933–34

A1: SA-Scharführer, SA-Feldjägerkorps

A corporal of the Sturmabteilung Feldjägerkorps, which acted as auxiliary police in the uncertain early days of the Nazi government. The uniform in SA olive-brown was cut similarly to that of the Prussian Police; police features included the brass star badge on the kepi and right collar patch, a duty gorget, and the Police bayonet, at this date bearing the Police star on the grip. The FJK distinguishing colour of white was displayed on the kepi, collar patches, piping to the collar, cuff and front edge of the tunic, and the underlay to the single, narrow, checkered white-and-black right shoulder strap. The single 'pip' of this rank is centred on the left collar patch, and the Party armband is worn on his left sleeve. Their auxiliary police role entitled the FJK to carry pistols – in this case a small Walther PPK.

A2: Oberwachtmeister, Bavarian Landespolizei

This long-service senior NCO's cap and tunic are still in the distinctive blueish-green colour worn before the introduction of the standardized grey-green of the Ordnungspolizei; it has black facings at the cap band, collar and cuffs, and bright green piping. The Police eagle is worn on the cap, but note that a silver-grey Army-style national emblem has been added to the right breast of the tunic since the Nazis came to power. He retains his Landespolizei shoulder straps and

ABOVE **A Police senior NCO in summer uniform, wearing the white-topped cap authorized in 1937 with a lightweight white tunic and grey-green breeches; shoulder straps were attached, but not collar patches. Traffic police also used white tunics for visibility, but were more often seen in long white duster coats to protect their uniforms when on point duty. (Josef Charita)**

silver cuff braid of rank; the collar bears silver-grey *Litzen* with bright green 'lights', and note also the green marksmanship lanyard from his right shoulder. In 1934–36 the Police bayonet had a clamshell guard; it is frogged to his belt with its decorative *Troddel* knot.

A3: Jäger, Landespolizeigruppe General Göring

This unit – eventually to evolve into the Luftwaffe's elite Division 'Hermann Göring' – was formed by Göring as Prussian Police President in February 1933 in order to create a crack police battalion of complete political reliability during the period when the Nazis were consolidating their power. In 1933–34 the members received military rank titles. The Landespolizei grey-green uniform was faced dark green on the collar only, and piped in bright green (including the cuffs and trouser seams). In December 1933 the unit was authorized a dark green cuff title with silver-grey edges and Gothic script 'L.P.G. General Göring'. This man wears the cross strap fitted to his black belt, with its circular swastika

LEFT **Schutzpolizei junior rank wearing the M1935 steel helmet and the regulation Police greatcoat – see Plate D1. The deep fall collar is faced dark brown and piped with bright green; shoulder straps were attached, but not collar patches or the Police sleeve eagle. He also wears a single set of leather triple ammunition pouches on his belt; this was normal for policemen in other than combat units who were issued the Mauser Kar 98k rifle. (Josef Charita)**

Like the Army mountain troops, the Hochgebirgs Gendarmerie – see Plate D3 – often found that ponies or mules were a more efficient means of transport than motor vehicles in the high country. This man wears the Police mountain cap with a metal national emblem, the trousers of the Wehrmacht's reversible grey/white winter oversuit, some kind of collarless padded overjacket, and a civilian scarf. (Josef Charita)

clasp, and the Police bayonet. Note the bronze *SA-Wehrabzeichen* on his left breast, worn by many policemen to mark their paramilitary training by the SA. In September 1935 the LPG was transferred to the Luftwaffe and retitled as a regiment.

B: UNIFIED NATIONAL POLICE, 1937–43
B1: Oberstleutnant, Schutzpolizei, c.1938 (Paradeanzug)
This lieutenant-colonel wears the parade dress introduced in 1937, with the officers' white horsehair plume attached to his shako; the parade waist and pouch belts in silver wire brocade with interwoven lines of black and red; officer's parade aiguillettes, and his full medals. The officer's shako has black leather peaks and crown, and fine quality silver wire and silvered metal furniture. His grey-green *Waffenrock* is faced with dark brown and piped bright green; the *Litzen* on his bright green collar patches, and the Police eagle on his left sleeve, are worked in silver wire thread for officers, and his shoulder straps are in silver cord on bright green underlay. The *Ehrenwinkel* chevron on his right sleeve indicates that he is an 'alte Kämpfer' – a member of the Nazi Party since before 30 January 1933. He carries the Police officer's sword and knot – *Degen mit*

Faustriemen – on a strap emerging under his pocket flap from a concealed inner belt.
B2: Leutnant standard-bearer, Schutzpolizei; Berlin, 1937 (Paradeanzug)
On 12 September 1937, Hitler presented this Party-style standard to the Berlin police. The second lieutenant carrying it wears the same uniform as B1, but with the appropriate shoulder straps of his rank, and a Police duty gorget – in this case with gilt eagle and bosses; the standard-bearer's bandolier is of black leather faced with bright green cloth and silver brocade, and he wears white gauntlets.
B3: Generalleutnant der Ordnungspolizei, c.1940 (Meldeanzug)
This Police major-general wears Reporting Order, and his uniform resembles that of an Army general officer, though in Police grey-green with brown facings and bright green piping (as B1) and distinctions – note the green *Lampassen* on his breeches. As a general he also has gilt buttons; gilt insignia, cords and piping on his service cap; gold-on-green 'alt Larisch' collar patches; interwoven gold and silver wire cord shoulder straps on green underlay, with one rank pip; a gold wire Police sleeve eagle, and a gilt miniature of it on the grip of his sword (if he were in full parade dress, he would also wear the brocade belt with a gilt clasp). Note on his left breast pocket, above his World War I Iron Cross First Class and Wound Badge, a Nazi Party member's badge; and below them, the silver embroidered SS-runes denoting his parallel membership of that organization.

C1: Oberleutnant, Verwaltungspolizei, c.1941–43 (Ausgehanzug)
The officer's walking-out dress is worn by this first lieutenant of the Administrative Police: service cap, tunic without belt but with medal ribbons and pin-on awards where appropriate, straight trousers with piped seams, lace-up shoes, dress sword or dagger with knot, and (officially) white gloves. The administrative branch uniform differed from that of the Schupo only in having light grey piping and distinctions instead of bright green; but note the shoulder straps, with a carmine line showing above the light grey underlay.
C2: Major, Schutzpolizei, c.1941–43 (Dienstanzug)
The officer's service dress differed in including unpiped breeches and riding boots, grey kid gloves, and a pistol holstered on the belt – here a P08 (Luger). This angle illustrates the bright green piping and two buttons on the false skirt pockets of the Police *Waffenrock* tunic.
C3: Meister, Wasserschutzpolizei, 1939 (Ausgehanzug)
This senior NCO wears the naval-cut reefer jacket and straight trousers of his service; his rank entitles him to wear officer-style gold cords on the stiffened service cap, and, for walking-out dress, the officer's dagger on its brocade hangers (the latter was replaced by the Police sword during 1939.) Rank was displayed by a combination of shoulder straps and braid cuff rings, somewhat analogous to the rings worn by company sergeants-major in the armed services. The Meister's shoulder strap is of standard Police design, with bright yellow *Truppenfarbe*. The Police sleeve eagle and cuff rings are in bright yellow. This former seaman proudly displays his World War I U-boat service badge.

D: MUNICIPAL POLICE & GENDARMERIE, C.1941–43

D1: Hauptwachtmeister, Schutzpolizei der Gemeinden

This NCO, posted to command a few men in a large country village, wears the standard Police pattern greatcoat, faced at the collar only with dark brown; no collar patches or sleeve eagle are displayed. The piping, and that on his NCO-pattern undress service cap and shoulder straps of rank, is wine-red. He wears a holstered P08 on the standard black belt with silver Police buckle. Under the coat he wears straight grey-green trousers and jackboots.

D2: Oberleutnant, Motorisierte Gendarmerie

This young first lieutenant of the motorized branch of the rural police wears the Gendarmerie service uniform with the officer-pattern cuff title bearing the name of this branch in silver-grey between edges of the same colour. Note the Gendarmerie's lighter camel-brown facings and orange piping, and their brown leather equipment.

D3: Wachtmeister, Hochgebirgs Gendarmerie

The 'High Mountain Gendarmerie' wore the traditional mountain cap with orange crown piping; note that he has added the metal Police eagle. His tunic, with camel-brown facings and orange piping, displays the standard Police enlisted ranks' collar insignia: silver-grey *Litzen* on *Truppenfarbe* patches surrounded by narrow silver-grey twist cord. His long mountain trousers are retained inside his cleated mountain boots by an elastic under the instep. His mittens are home-knitted – the kind of personal touch that was tolerated. A typical ribbon bar might show those of the War Merit Cross with Swords, and the cornflower-blue long-service medal. This man has also served in the front line, as shown by the buttonhole ribbons of the 1939 Iron Cross Second Class and the Russian Front Winter 1941/42 medal, and by the General Assault Badge and the black Wound Badge – for the injury which no doubt keeps him on the home front now.

E: FIRE & AIR PROTECTION POLICE

E1: Wachtmeister, Feuerschutzpolizei, c.1938

The original Fire Protection Police uniform in dark blue has carmine (deep rose pink) piping and distinctions. Above the sleeve eagle the name of the Bezirk (district) is embroidered in an arc of Gothic lettering. The Fire Protection Police helmet has a sharp angle to the 'step' in front of the ear, and two pierced circles for ventilation on each side. A broad leather protective neck flap was normally fitted. Helmets were made both with and without a chromed fore-and-aft 'comb' over the skull; many were later fitted with a Y-shaped chinstrap. The special wide belt has a large steel 'karabiner' or snap hook at the left front, mounted on a plate riveted to the belt; a hatchet case hangs below the left hip.

E2: Hauptmann, Feuerschutzpolizei, 1938–42

This officer wears the grey-green Police service dress introduced during 1938, with black facings at cap band, collar and cuffs; this was changed to standard dark brown during 1942. The piping and distinctions are still carmine, and as an officer he wears the sleeve eagle in silver thread. In his buttonhole is the ribbon of the 1939 War Service Cross Second Class, and on his pocket the First Class decoration with Swords for bravery; this series of crosses was widely awarded for service not in actual combat.

A factory guard of the Werkschutz – see also Plate F3. There was little standardization of uniform, and a wide range of differently cut and coloured military-style tunics and breeches were worn with peaked caps and jackboots. This watchman poses in a smart combination of pale tunic and medium-tone cap, perhaps in shades of grey, with dark breeches. The tunic displays plain collar patches, shoulder straps, and a *'Werkschutz'* cufftitle in Latin block script, probably in silver-grey on a dark red band. Note also the whistle lanyard and holstered Walther PPK pistol; under magnification a medal ribbon with crossed swords motif can also be made out.

E3: Zugführer, Luftschutzpolizei, 1942–45

This junior officer of Air Protection Police, of equivalent rank to Leutnant, is in undress order; he wears that service's uniform of Luftwaffe cut and colour inherited from the Sicherheits und Hilfssdienst, with officer's silver piping on the cap and upper collar. His Police cap and left-sleeve insignia are also in that colour. The collar patches show silver embroidered *Litzen* with dark green 'lights' on black backing; and the narrow shoulder straps, on black underlay, are unusual in having a single green cord inset from the long edges – a feature carried over from the SHD, from part of which the Luftschutzpolizei was created.

The 1942-pattern insignia for Police generals – see Plate G3. This is SS-Gruppenführer und Generalleutant der Polizei Kurt Göhrum, the Police President of Berlin, who displays SS-pattern ranking in gold on police-green collar patches on his dark brown collar facing. (Josef Charita)

F: TN, RAILWAY & FACTORY POLICE

F1: TN-Bereitschaftsführer, Technische Nothilfe, 1942

This engineer, of a grade equivalent to Leutnant, wears officers' distinctions on the field-grey uniform that was steadily replacing the pre-war dark blue, as increasing numbers of the membership served with the armed forces. Note the solid diamond-shaped swastika on the national cap badge, and the Army-style wreath and cockade on the black cap band; the cap piping is plain silver. The original photo shows this opened tunic collar, following that of the blue uniform; others show enlisted men in the conventional Army field blouse with closed collar. The insignia are those used from 1941 to 1943; the subject photo shows mirror-image collar patches of rank (in 1937–41 all but the three most senior ranks, from TN-Landesführer upwards, displayed detachment numbers on the right-hand patch). The rectangular black patches bear an aluminium cogwheel, above embroidered wire laurel sprays showing this series of ranks; the edging is flecked with black. The narrow shoulder straps are of plain silver cord on black underlay. Note the TeNo eagle on its triangular backing, set high on the left sleeve, and the cuff title on the left forearm. This man's ribbons show that he has seen service with the Wehrmacht in Russia in the first winter of the campaign.

F2: Bzp-Oberabteilungsführer, Bahnschutzpolizei

This officer of the Railway Protection Police, equivalent to a Hauptmann, wears the closed-collar version of service dress. The cap crown and uniform are in this service's unique light blue-grey, with a dark blue-grey collar and cap band; cap piping and cords are silver, as are the insignia, featuring a special wreath incorporating the winged wheel. The collar patches are black, with the broad silver thread borders, winged wheel and single star of this rank. The shoulder straps are in silver cord flecked with black chevrons, on black underlay; above the single gilt rank pip (note that Bzp straps did not follow the usual military sequence) are a gilt unit number and winged wheel. The sleeve eagle is similar to the first pattern used by the SS-Verfügungstruppe. For this group of officer grades the Gothic 'Bahnschutzpolizei' cuff title is worked in black on silver brocade with darker silver edges. The winged wheel motif is repeated on the silver clasp of the black belt.

F3: Werkschutzpolizist, c.1944

Members of factory guard services wore a variety of uniforms usually in either blue or grey. About the only constants were the Werkschutzpolizei upper cap badge, and the oval left-sleeve badge with cord edging. The former features an eagle with a tilted shield at bottom left bearing a swastika; the latter, a stylized impression of a factory, between wings and above a half-cogwheel, the whole 'protected' by the same shield. Collar patches were issued by some factories, bearing their company logos; we have chosen to show here that of a Dortmund gas-processing plant, with a stylized 'KA' within 'D' monogram, but we have no way of knowing whether this patch was actually issued. The 'Werkschutz' cuff title is in light grey on carmine; and note this example of a kind of duty gorget, pinned to the tunic, bearing a white eagle and 'Werkschutz' scroll on a red-painted background.

G: PRISONS, POSTAL PROTECTION & POLICE GENERAL

G1: Strafanstaltbeamte, prison service, 1940

This prison official in service dress is of a grade roughly equivalent to a Police Hauptwachtmeister, and serves as a senior warder in an ordinary criminal prison or Strafgefängnis. The uniform is Police grey-green with dark green distinctions, gold 'lace and metal' and carmine piping. The cap cords are dark green with heavy gold flecking. The plain tunic-colour collar and cuffs are piped carmine; the special dark green collar patches are edged with gold cord and bear an ornate button. The shoulder straps have dark green central cords with two flower-shaped rank pips, gold outer cords flecked with bright green, and carmine underlay. Note that the belt clasp is slightly oval. Some examples of the tunic had a fly front concealing the buttons.

G2: Abteilungshauptführer, Postschutz, pre-1942

This official's grade entitles him to officer-style cap cords, shoulder straps, and a silver-grey sleeve eagle of the special Postschutz design, with the eagle and swastika overlaying triple lightning bolts. (However, note that our subject photo still shows an enlisted man's belt buckle.) The uniform is field-grey with dark green cap band and collar; the cap insignia are aluminium, and the wreath of the cockade is of a special design incorporating the lightning-bolts. The orange distinctions of the postal service appear in the piping of the cap and of the trousers worn for walking-out dress; the shoulder strap underlay; the edging of the mid-green collar patches; and the Gothic lettering 'Postschutz' on the light grey cuff band. The silver rank insignia worn on the collar patches are already of SS style; from March 1942 the Postschutz was transferred from the Ministry of Post and Telegraph into the Allgemeine-SS, and adopted full SS collar and sleeve insignia. Like so many uniformed organizations, the Postal police had a special dagger for wear with walking-out uniforms, with the Postschutz national emblem on the black grip. This man displays a Party membership badge.

G3: Generaloberst der Ordnungspolizei, 1944

This figure is based on photos of SS-Obstgruf u. GenObst der Polizei Kurt Daluege, executive head of the Ordnungspolizei 1934–42, and nominally until the end of the war. It shows the final pattern of Police general's rank insignia worn from late 1942, embroidered to SS rather than Army design. This colonel-general wears an undress uniform, and follows fashion in having his tunic tailored with the collar opened to wear over a shirt collar and tie – and, in this case, the Knight's Cross of the War Service Cross with Swords at his throat. The general officers' shoulder straps are of gold and silver interwoven cord on bright green underlay, with the three small silver pips of this rank set one above two; the sleeve eagle is in heavy gold wire embroidery. Among his decorations Daluege displayed the German Cross in Silver on his right breast, and on his left a Gold Party Badge above the War Service Cross First Class with Swords, and his Wound Badge from World War I. The embroidered silver-thread SS-runes on a grey-green backing mark his parallel membership of that organization, in which he also held the rank of colonel-general. The undress uniform trousers have bright green Lampassen.

H: ARMED POLICE, 1943–45

H1: Wachtmeister, Schutzpolizei, c.1943

This Schupo NCO wears the much plainer Army-style Feldbluse tunic introduced in 1943 to replace the more elaborate and expensive Waffenrock as the normal service dress. The brown facings and green piping have disappeared, and the collar Litzen are woven on plain, unedged, bright green patches; the shoulder straps and sleeve eagle are unchanged. He wears straight trousers confined by canvas anklets over ankle boots. The field cap has the unique Police piping, up the front and along both crests of the top fold; the Police insignia is woven in silver-grey on black. He carries a Kar 98k service rifle and a single set of its ammunition pouches, but has not been issued the decorative Police bayonet. His aluminium duty gorget is unchanged.

H2: Meister, Schutzpolizei armoured troops, 1944

The crews of Police light armoured vehicles – usually captured foreign types, issued to some Barracked Police internal security units from 1942 – were authorized the Army-style black 'special uniform for armour crews'. The Police version, as worn by this warrant officer, had bright green piping round the collar, and a green-on-black sleeve eagle with a white swastika. His collar patches and his shoulder straps of rank are conventional: the former with silver-grey Litzen on bright green backing edged with silver-grey cord, and the latter of diagonally interwoven dark brown and silver cords, surrounded by silver cords, the silver flecked with dark brown chevrons, all on bright green underlay. Black Schiffchen and M1943 Einheitsfeldmütze field caps were both produced, with silver-grey Police eagles woven on black backing, and here with bright green crown seam

A number of policemen were highly decorated for combat service. Here, Oberst der Schutzpolizei Bernhard Griese wears the M1943 cap, piped silver at the crown seam and bearing a metal cockade above a woven Police eagle. His plain field tunic displays the Knight's Cross at the throat (awarded May 1942), the Eastern Winter Campaign 1941/42 ribbon in the buttonhole, and on his left breast the Iron Cross First Class, Infantry Assault Badge, Wound Badge, War Service Cross with Swords First Class, and a number of other decorations from World War I and its aftermath. (Josef Charita)

piping. This man, who has clearly served in the occupied territories, displays both classes of the Iron Cross and the bronze Anti-Partisan War Badge.

H3: Oberwachtmeister, Schutzpolizei, 1945

This NCO, serving in the war zone that was remorselessly advancing into Germany, wears the Police version of the Waffen-SS so-called 'pea-pattern' non-reversible four-pocket combat uniform; the box-pleated breast pockets are the only difference from the W-SS issue that is apparent in photographs. His shoulder straps are the only insignia attached. He wears the old Schiffchen field cap (which was seen worn alongside the M1943 visored cap throughout the war), in this case made of standard field-grey cloth rather than Police grey-green, and lacking the bright green Police piping. In the chaos of the collapsing Third Reich the only rifle available to his unit is the obsolete Gewehr 98.

INDEX

Figures in **bold** refer to illustrations.